HOW TO WRITE
FOR CHILDREN

Other Allison & Busby Writers' Guides

HOW TO WRITE FOR CHILDREN

Tessa Krailing

a&b

First published in Great Britain in 1988 by
Allison & Busby Ltd
114 New Cavendish Street
London W1M 7FD
http://www.allisonandbusby.ltd.uk

Reprinted 1996, 2000

A catalogue record for this book is available from
the British Library.

ISBN 0 7490 0258 1

Typeset by DAG Publications Ltd, London.
Printed and bound in Great Britain by
Biddles Ltd, Guildford.

CONTENTS

Acknowledgements

ACKNOWLEDGEMENTS

The Author and the Publishers would like to thank the following for the use of copyright material:

Beverley Anderson, The Good Book Guide to Children's Books 1986; The Bodley Head for an extract from *Babies Need Books* by Dorothy Butler: copyright © Dorothy Butler 1980; Hamish Hamilton Ltd and The Putnam Young Readers Group for examples taken from *Princess Smartypants* by Babette Cole: copyright © 1986 by Babette Cole; Hutchinson Children's Books for an extract from *Message from Venus* by Tessa Krailing: copyright © Tessa Krailing 1996.

The author would also like to thank Gwynneth Ashby, Dianne and Stanley Doubtfire, John Escott, Shirley Hughes, Diana Kimpton, Geoffrey Lamb, Brenda Little, Fiona Reynoldson, Ann Thwaite and Valerie Wilding for their help, advice and encouragement.

WHY WRITE FOR CHILDREN

Why write for children?

Well, there's really only one possible motive for any kind of writing: namely, that there's a book inside you demanding to be written and you won't be happy until it's safely down on paper. It doesn't matter whether that book is a learned philosophical treatise or a picture story for five-year-olds, the compulsion is the same.

Is that the case with you?

Perhaps at this stage "compulsion" may seem too strong a word. Perhaps you have an idea for a story that you want to write for children, but you are not sure how to tackle it. What you are looking for is guidance, some practical advice that will help you crystallise your idea into an entertaining, well-crafted, and – with luck – saleable children's book. So here goes.

Let's start by exploding a few myths.

First, that children's books are easier to write than adult novels. Not true, I'm afraid. Admittedly the structure and the language you use may be simpler than for an adult novel, but simplicity is not always easy to achieve. As in most myths, there's an element of truth in that the books may be shorter, although not necessarily so. However the quality of the writing required is certainly no lower than for an adult novel and may in some respects be higher. It is not a lesser art, merely a different one.

Myth number two: that it is easier to get a children's book published than an adult novel. Again, there's a tiny grain of truth here: these days the adult fiction market is so rigidly structured that it is increasingly difficult to break into it with a slightly off-beat idea. The children's book market is more flexible. There is still room for the writer whose book doesn't quite fit into any particular genre. All publishers, though, are notoriously reluctant to take risks, so you'll have to convince at least one of them that you have something new and interesting to offer which is worth a little risk-taking.

Myth number three: that it is a good idea to start your literary career by writing for children and work your way up. Fatal. If it's an adult novel you're burning to write, then go ahead and do it. You'll never write a good children's book unless you put your heart and soul into it, so it's no use keeping the best of yourself in reserve for something you intend doing later on.

Myth number four: that most children's writers are failed adult novelists anyway. Then how about Penelope Lively, Nina Bawden, Jane Gardam, Roald Dahl, Peter Dickinson, Joan Aiken, to name but a few? Become a children's writer and you will find yourself in excellent company.

Now, having dispelled some of the myths, let's take a look at the more positive reasons why you should want to write for children.

An indelible impression

If you ask people to name their three favourite books the chances are that at least one of those three will be a children's book. According to his biographer, Noel Coward's lifelong favourite was E. Nesbit's *The Enchanted Castle*. It was found open on his bedside table the night he died. The books we read and loved when we were young leave an indelible impression on us. In some curious and subtle way they have entered our subconscious.

Here is the opening of *The Wind in the Willows*:

> The Mole had been working very hard all the morning, spring-cleaning his little home. First with brooms, then with dusters; then on ladders and steps and chairs, with a brush and a pail of whitewash; till he had dust in his throat and eyes, and splashes of whitewash all over his black fur, and an aching back and weary arms. Spring was moving in the air above and in the earth below and around him, penetrating even his dark and

lowly little house with its spirit of divine discontent and longing. It was small wonder, then, that he suddenly flung down his brush on the floor, said "Bother!" and "O blow!" and also "Hang spring-cleaning" and bolted out of the house without even waiting to put on his coat.

I have only to read those words to feel a tingling sense of anticipation. Something's coming and it's going to be good. I can depend upon this book to transport me into another world where I shall be entertained and entranced and sometimes a little scared. Above all, I shall be with friends I've known for a very long time, friends I can trust.

I don't feel a bit like that about the adult novel I read last week, enjoyable though it was. These days I'm not so impressionable. Too many other factors have entered my life, clouding that intensity of vision I had as a child and making it more difficult for me to enter other worlds. The only way I can recapture those sensations is by taking my old friends down from the bookshelf and blowing the dust off their jackets.

Why is it that children have this remarkable ability to lose themselves totally in the world of the imagination?

Mainly, I think, it is because their minds are so fresh and receptive. There hasn't yet been time for them to get clogged up with the many drives and anxieties of adult life. Still free spirits, they can move easily between fantasy and reality without being in any danger of confusing the two worlds. But whichever world they inhabit, they are constantly absorbing new ideas and information. Everything they see, hear, read or watch on television is making that indelible mark that will probably last, if only subconsciously, for the rest of their lives.

Which means that the book you are about to write may well play a significant part in the formation of someone's character.

What a responsibility!

Perhaps it is best not to think about that too much. It could be inhibiting. The point I'm trying to make is that children's books *matter*. They are important. Second-best just won't do in this field, as indeed in any other when it comes to writing. You have to go for gold.

The child inside

Do you have a clear mental picture of the child for whom you are writing your story? Perhaps it is your own son or daughter. Or your grandchild. Or one of the children you teach, if you happen to be a teacher.

Forget them all.

I wrote my first children's book while I was still teaching. My class of nine-year-olds were mad about dinosaurs and always clamouring for stories about them, so rather rashly I said I would write one. Driving home from school I hatched up an idea about a lady dinosaur called Minerva, who was alive and well and had been living for the past few million years under the Mendip Hills. Only now she had developed toothache ...

Well, it was a starting point. The strange thing was that as soon as I began to write I lost sight of the children in my class altogether. I was writing this for *me*! And it was with this realisation that the story really caught fire.

The trouble is that if you try writing objectively, for some child or children "out there", it is all too easy to fall into the trap of writing *down* to your readers. Try as hard as you may, a note of condescension creeps in, bringing with it a sense of distance between you and them. Next thing you know, you are toppling over the edge into that awful tweeness or cosiness which typifies the worst kind of children's writing. And children can spot insincerity a mile off. They are not fooled for an instant.

So the child you should really be writing for is the child inside yourself, that part of you still capable of wonder and enthusiasm and imaginative leaps into fantasy. It's important, of course, not to confuse being child*like* with being child*ish*. It's that freshness of vision you're after, the ability to see things as if for the first time instead of through a fog of world-weary adult cynicism. Difficult? Not necessarily.

That same class of nine-year-olds had listened enthralled to C.S. Lewis's *The Lion, the Witch and the Wardrobe*, which I read to them during the autumn term. At Christmas we worked together on a huge picture covering one wall of the classroom, depicting the moment when Santa Claus arrives in Narnia in defiance of the White Witch. We painted the background and stuck on everything bright we could find – cotton-wool snow sprinkled with glitter, foil-covered parcels on the sleigh, and a mass of silver stars in the sky. When it was finished the headmaster came to see what we'd done. The children and I waited, holding our breath, for his verdict.

"Very nice," he said at last. "Gaudy, but nice."

When he'd gone the children asked me what "gaudy" meant.

"Brilliant," I said. "Brightly-coloured. Sparkling."

They were quite happy with that. But I had just had a profound revelation. Up to that moment I had been looking at that picture through a child's eyes and it wasn't until an adult came into the room that I was forced to see it in a different light. Yes, it *was* gaudy. Unashamedly, eye-dazzlingly, over-the-top gaudy. But the children and I had thought it was beautiful. It was, I think, at this point that I realised that part of me had never stopped being a child. I make no apologies for the fact. It has stood me in very good stead.

Ah, you may well – and very sensibly – say, but isn't there a danger here? If I write for the child I once was won't my writing be dated? Children have changed. They live in a very different world from the one I inhabited when I was young and are subject to totally different influences. How can I be sure that what I write will still be relevant?

Two points. The first is that I never suggested you should write for the child you *once were*. That would be a mistake. It is the child still alive inside you now, the one who's travelled all the way with you since those early years, that you should be aiming at.

Second, emotions don't change. If you can recall on paper your own feelings of fear, happiness, excitement, loneliness, insecurity and love, then you can climb inside the skin of any modern child or adolescent. The externals don't matter so much – they can be easily researched. It's what goes on inside your characters' hearts and minds that counts.

Dual standards

There is one factor in writing for children that doesn't occur in other kinds of fiction, and that's the necessity to please not only the readership you are aiming at but also the adults who stand between you and that readership. By this I mean publishers and booksellers as well as the parents, grandparents, aunts, uncles, teachers etc who you hope will buy your book. Unless *they* like your work it may never reach the audience it's intended for.

Is this need to operate on two levels at once a real problem?

I don't believe it is. It seems to me that if a book is "true", in the sense that it's honest and written from the heart, then its appeal will be universal. Many highly successful books have attracted a far wider range of readers than their authors could at first have imagined. Look at Tolkien's *Lord of the Rings* or Sue Townsend's *Adrian Mole* books. The practice of labelling books as suitable for specific age groups is largely a marketing device, since a bright eight-year-old can easily cope with a book intended for an older child. Conversely, a fourteen-year-old may still derive enormous pleasure from re-reading a book he first enjoyed when he was nine.

Come to that, so may a forty-year-old. To my mind, the test of a good children's book is that it should appeal to readers of all ages. This is certainly true of the classics and is surely the reason why the *The Secret Garden* and the *William* books are still read and enjoyed today.

In any case none of these considerations should enter your head when you start writing. My experience is that a book will find its own level, so it simply isn't worth worrying about. *To thine own (writing) self be true*, and let instinct be your guide.

Are you sitting comfortably?

Then we're almost ready to begin. I have just one suggestion to make, that you should visit the children's section of your local library and take a look at some of the books which have been published in the last ten years.

You may find it quite an eye-opener.

There is no need to attempt an in-depth survey of the entire range of current children's literature. Just borrow a few books you like the look of and read them purely for pleasure. However, if you feel in need of guidance, a recommended reading list can be found at the back of this book. Or ask your local librarian.

Be careful, though. Even if you find an author you admire tremendously, don't allow him/her to influence you too much. The last thing you want to do is try to imitate other writers, since your best hope of success lies in being different from everyone else. Developing your own unique style, seeing things with a fresh eye – that is what writing is all about.

2

WHAT KIND OF A STORY?

By far the greatest part of this book will be concerned with the writing of fiction. As Ann Thwaite – herself an author of both fiction and non-fiction – says: "Books about castles or transport or the weather are useful, of course, but they can only teach the child about castles or transport or the weather – whereas good fiction, good stories, can tell a child about human relationships and the possibilities of life itself and other things far more important than castles, transport and the weather."

First you need to decide what kind of a story you want to write. Inevitably your choice will be influenced by your own tastes and interests. For example, if you enjoy reading mysteries, the chances are that you'll be on the same wavelength as the child who also loves mysteries. If your passion is sport then why not try your hand at a story about football or swimming or tennis? The greatest mistake you could make would be to choose, say, science fiction because you've heard that it sells well, even though you're only slightly interested in the subject and have little or no specialist knowledge.

It may be useful to consider some of the main headings under which publishers tend to categorise books. There are, of course, many books that defy categorisation, so this is not a definitive list, merely a rough guide.

Animal stories

These have always been popular with children. Tales about horses, dogs, cats, deer, bears, even gerbils have found favour over the years, and their hold shows no sign of weakening. There's such a wealth of animal stories available, however, that if you want to break into this field you need to have something really fresh and lively to offer. To write about the real-life adventures of your pet dog, however amusing they may seem to you, may not strike a publisher as being different enough for him to take a chance on it – unless of course you're Frank Muir writing about What-a-mess.

And therein lies the irony. As soon as a subject is dismissed as "overworked", the chances are that someone will come along and make a nonsense of that statement. Just when everyone had decided there was no more mileage in talking rabbits, Richard Adams proved them wrong by writing *Watership Down*. And although the purists may say that animals should always be depicted behaving as animals do behave and in their natural habitat – that is, not wearing funny clothes and living in houses and talking to humans – you have only to see a child devouring the *Paddington* books to realise that this is being pedantic.

Animal stories can be divided into two main types: those about real animals acting in a realistic manner – *Black Beauty* and *Tarka the Otter* are classic examples of this genre – and those which pretend to be about animals but are in fact about humans in disguise. This last seems to me a perfectly valid form of storytelling, since it enables children to identify with the central character and share his adventures once removed. In one of the best children's books ever written, E.B. White's *Charlotte's Web*, Wilbur the pig is in grave danger of being slaughtered and is only saved by the ingenuity of Charlotte the spider. This situation could easily be disturbing for children but, although they're naturally concerned for Wilbur, they feel sufficiently distanced by the animal device to be able to cope with it.

Possibly the greatest hazard when writing about animals is that it is all too easy, when describing a small and endearing creature, to lapse into sentimentality. Use of the world "little" seems to constitute a particular danger. "The mouse shed a tear" is one thing; "The mouse shed a *little* tear" quite another.

One kind of animal story currently enjoying a revival is the pony book, so – provided you're familiar with horses and know your snaffle from your martingale – the world is your stable.

9

Fairytale, myth and legend

Stories about fairies *as such* are not in fashion right now. It may well be that you know children who still lap them up, and of course there's always a chance you'll come up with something so refreshingly different that a publisher will jump at it. Nonetheless most children over the age of six groan at the mere mention of fairies, elves and pixies, possibly because they associate them with the nauseatingly twee style of storytelling that used to be thought appropriate. In my opinion this does a grave disservice to the world of faery; but if you are determined to venture into this field I suggest you go back to its roots and try to find a completely new approach.

The re-telling of ancient myths and folk-tales always delights children – no danger of tweeness here – but there's already a wealth of beautifully illustrated books covering the best known areas. If, however, you have a collection of stories from a part of the world which has been less well documented, then it's certainly worth having a go. Or, like Terry Jones with *The Saga of Erik the Viking*, you can invent your own mythological world, which seems authentic but isn't.

Myths and folk-tales in a modern form have been the inspiration for both adult and children's literature. The story of Cinderella, for example, is one of the most irresistible plots in the world and the variety of interpretations writers can put upon it is seemingly inexhaustible. Adèle Geras, in her trilogy about three girls at boarding school, has taken three well-known fairy-tales and transformed them into magical modern love stories. *The Tower Room*, for example, is based on the story of Rapunzel; *Watching the Roses* on the Sleeping Beauty; and *Pictures of the Night* on Snow White and the Seven Dwarfs. The possibilities seem endless. All you need is a fresh eye.

Mystery and adventure

This is possibly the broadest stream in children's fiction, embracing everything that sets out primarily to tell a thumping good story.

But is it pure escapism?

At one end of the scale it undoubtedly is, transporting the reader to a world quite outside his own experience, and none the worse for that. As a child I read Arthur Ransome's *Swallows and Amazons* over and over again, revelling in the exploits of children who lived a far more active and independent life than I did. The fact that I knew nothing about sailing and hadn't a clue what cleats and halyards and thwarts were didn't matter one bit. That was all part of the fascination. Escapism it may have been, but I believe it also widened my horizons.

When writing a mystery you start with an enormous advantage, since most children love the puzzle element in a story and can't resist the challenge of trying to solve it. There is, however, a subtle but important difference between mystery and crime, where you inevitably run into difficulties if you let your child characters become involved with dangerous criminals. These may, of course, be comic criminals; but if they are in any way realistic it can be difficult to make the children's ultimate victory over them believable. To have the police take over in the last chapter, charging to the rescue like the US cavalry, is a terrible let-down for the reader. So is the discovery that the mysterious wooden box everyone has been making such a fuss about contains the inevitable cache of stolen jewels or banknotes or contraband. Far more interesting, to my mind, are mysteries about *people* – why they lie and cheat and occasionally act in a way that seems entirely out of character. If there's a crime involved then let it be understandable in human terms and not merely a device of the plot.

Perhaps the chief danger in this particular genre is the temptation to devise the plot first and put the characters in later. This inevitably results in weak characterisation; and although children may still read and enjoy the story, it won't make the lasting impression on them that a more fully conceived book would have done.

Ghost and horror

Testing our resistance to fear is a part of growing up. From the Grimm brothers onwards, gruesome tales have always held a particular fascination for the young – and never more so than at the present time. In fact this has become such a popular genre in the last few years that publishers are always ready to consider new material. It is advisable, though, to avoid the cliché situation, such as old haunted houses and grey ladies drifting through the corridors at midnight.

When it comes to horror the question arises, How far should you go? In other words, where do you draw the line between permissible nastiness and what is likely to be genuinely disturbing? Perhaps it's worth bearing in mind that most people are far more afraid of the Unknown, the unseen horror in the dark, than by what they can see. In most horror movies the monsters are at their most frightening when they're invisible, a threatening presence just outside the door, but as soon as they appear with their crinkly plastic skin and bulging foreheads they are just plain ludicrous. It's the anticipation that makes the child hide behind the sofa, not the reality.

Clearly, though, you have a moral obligation here, especially when writing for younger children. In the end Good must be shown to triumph over Evil, Light over Dark. That is the certainty which makes it possible for a child to test his courage, secure in his belief that the world is basically an orderly, benevolent place. If this goes against the artistic grain, then perhaps you should be writing horror stories for adults, not children.

School stories

This is another perennially popular field. A school is a microcosm, where children experience many of the joys and perplexities they will have to cope with in adult life. It therefore provides a situation rich in possibilities for conflict, humour and self-discovery and many writers have made good use of it in many different ways. Michael Coleman, in *Triv in Pursuit* has the entire teaching staff of St Ethelred's mysteriously disappearing one-by-one; and in my own *Miranda at War* Miranda takes a strong dislike to her unsympathetic new teacher, Mr Duffy, and decides he must be made to go.

Remember, though, that this is a field in which all children are experts. So be sure you get your facts right, and strive for the ring of authenticity that will make your story credible. If you are a parent yourself you probably have a pretty good idea what goes on in schools today; and if you're a teacher, even better. It shouldn't be too difficult to put yourself on the other side of the fence.

Fantasy

Make-believe is not merely a game to a child, it's a serious business. Watch any group of children at play and they will almost certainly be acting out a fantasy, with as many rules and regulations as any adult society can dream up. Like tiger cubs pouncing on an imaginary prey, they are preparing for life.

Fantasy is by its very nature impossible to define. It can be humorous and cosy; or it can be on an epic, mythological scale. It can take as its starting point the invasion of magic into our familiar, everyday world; or it can be about other worlds and other times. For the writer it offers an enormously rich field of possibility. We are into the realms of "What if ...?" which means there are virtually no restraints on your creativity. Anything goes, provided of course you can make it credible.

Some writers take normality as their starting point, placing children in a recognisably real setting before they introduce the fantastical element. P.L. Travers' *Mary Poppins* is a good example – it is worth reading the original book if you've only seen the film – and so is E. Nesbitt's *Five Children and It*, in which the Psammead, a Sand Fairy, appears with the power to grant wishes. The attraction of this kind of story is that young readers can easily imagine themselves in a similar situation. How interesting life would be if the old rug on the living-room floor were to become a magic carpet; or if an unpopular teacher turned out to be a witch in disguise.

A bonus of this genre is the opportunity it offers for humour. You have only to introduce one unlikely factor to open up a whole new area of comic possibility. Roald Dahl is a writer who has explored this field to great effect. In *James and the Giant Peach*, from the moment James escapes from his unpleasant aunts through a tunnel leading to the centre of an enormous peach, the story takes off into the realms of wild and often hilarious imagination.

Alice falling down the rabbit-hole to find herself in a world that rapidly became curiouser and curiouser was undoubtedly the point when fantasy fiction really took off. By taking a child out of her familiar setting and placing her in a totally unfamiliar one, Lewis Carroll hit on an idea that has been fascinating writers – and readers – ever since.

The method of transition from reality to fantasy is a good test of a writer's ingenuity. The four children in C.S. Lewis's *The Lion, the Witch and the Wardrobe* discover Narnia by accident when one of them hides in a wardrobe. In Alan Garner's *Elidor* the four children find their way into the kingdom of Elidor through an old church on a demolition site in Manchester. In each case the method of transition helps to set the pattern, as when Alice stepped through the looking glass to find herself in a mirror world. What happens next will inevitably reflect the main preoccupations of you, the writer.

The possibility of a character slipping out of his own time into another has also proved a fruitful source of inspiration. If you've ever stood on the ramparts of Carisbrooke Castle, or in the shadows of Stonehenge, and wished you could be transported back in time, you'll be aware of the story possibilities that lie in exploring the fourth dimension. Most children have a strong sense of history, although it's worth remembering, when writing for the very young, that the actual time scale doesn't mean a great deal. 1066 and 1812 are much the same as far as a seven-year-old is concerned. Prehistory, though, has an endless fascination for them, and they can make the imaginative time-leap from the present day to the Stone Age with no difficulty at all.

Going one step further, you may prefer to leave the real world behind altogether and take your readers into new and uncharted territory. Here you are totally in command: you can create new planets, new societies, new religions. Before letting all this power go to your head, however, it is as well to remember that, however strange your imaginary world may be, your readers will need something they can recognise, some points of reference they can hang on to. Otherwise they may find it all too confusing and lose interest.

As you can see, the scope is limitless. All you need is to find a fresh approach, bearing in mind that friendly dragons, witches-in-disguise and bumbling giants have been rather overworked.

But if you take the invasion of magic as your starting point it isn't hard to imagine the kind of havoc that can follow even in this material age – perhaps *especially* in this material age. And if it leads to enlightenment as well, then you'll have produced a satisfying book.

One word of warning. It was all right for Lewis Carroll to make Alice escape by waking up since he was probably the first to think of it. But if you end a story now with the words, "After all, it was only a dream!" your reader will close the book with a deep and heartfelt groan of disappointment.

Science fiction

Where do you draw the line between fantasy and science fiction?

The word "science" implies knowledge that is proven; taken in conjunction with the word "fiction" it suggests a kind of conjectural literature, starting with known facts about the world we live in and using them as a basis for prophecy. Science fiction, then, is primarily about the future as the writer imagines it will be. If it takes a trip into the past it is only by means of a future invention, such as H.G. Wells's time machine or Dr Who's Tardis.

It is when science fiction ventures into space that you may, when writing specifically for children, come up against certain difficulties. The chief stumbling block is characterisation, since, if you are going for credibility, your astronauts will be adults. This is perfectly acceptable – after all, there are no children aboard the starship Enterprise – but you do have to be on your guard against portraying them as immature, overgrown kids. It is all too easy to end up with a kind of Famous Five in Space. Another difficulty is presented by the hardware: if you want to make your spacecraft believable then you must obviously be familiar with the kind of jargon that will give it that touch of authenticity. The child who enjoys space fiction will be fairly knowledgeable on the subject, so it is no use being vague and hoping for the best.

If you have a strong desire to write in this genre the chances are that you are already a devotee of SF, in which case you won't need me to tell you the wide variety of story ideas and treatment available to you. However, it is worth bearing in mind that, despite the scientific trappings, space fiction works best when it is based firmly in the mainstream of children's narrative literature. While making use of the ever-popular elements of adventure, horror, fantasy and myth, the successful writer is the one who sets out primarily to tell a thumping good story.

Historical novels

It is often said that historical novels don't sell well these days because children are more interested in the future than they are in the past. Well, there may be some truth in that. But it is interesting to note that some of the most talented and prestigious writers of children's fiction are to be found in this field – Geoffrey Trease, Rosemary Sutcliffe, Leon Garfield, Henry Treece and Jill Paton Walsh among others.

These are, of course, highly intelligent, articulate writers, and it is inevitable that their books should appeal primarily to highly intelligent, articulate children. This seems to me only fair and just. These days, thank goodness, a great many books are produced specifically to suit the less able child, but we shouldn't forget that the exceptionally bright and able reader also needs to be catered for. So if you decide to write an historical novel you'll find a select but appreciative readership awaiting you.

This readership, however, is used to – and therefore has come to expect – only the best. It is no use thinking that, just because you're writing for children, you can skimp on research. Children who are interested in history often acquire a phenomenal knowledge of their particular period and will be quick to spot any kind of inaccuracy.

Humour

Although humour can be found in all categories, especially fantasy, there is an area where it exists in its own right. I'm thinking not only of *Just William* but also of the *Ramona* stories of Beverley Cleary and Dorothy Edward's *My Naughty Little Sister*.

These are all collections of stories about children with whom any normal, grubby-kneed, accident-prone child can identify. They are often farcical, but never slip over the edge into whimsy. Moreover they have a freshness and vitality about them that doesn't seem to date, and which no doubt accounts for their continued popularity. If you have a well-developed sense of the ridiculous, and take pleasure in making people laugh, you may well find this a fruitful area to explore.

3

THE VITAL SPARK

The question most often asked of writers is, "Where do you get your ideas from?" It is also the question most likely to strike them dumb. The truth is that most writers don't really like talking about the source of their inspiration, even if they know what it is, for fear that one day the well of ideas may dry up altogether, leaving them without an original thought in their heads.

Very often, when we start writing for children, we tend to think, "Ah, now what would they like? A story about a fire engine? Or about a mouse? Or how about four children who meet on a camping holiday and have an adventure?" These are stories we pluck out of the air. Or, more accurately, they are stories we've read or heard somewhere and we've got it into our heads that they are the kind of things children want. They come from outside us, not from within us. And that means our story will inevitably be just like everybody else's stories. In other words, it will have predictable storybook characters and a stereotypical plot.

No, if we want to come up with something original we have to dig a little deeper than that. Dig into ourselves, in fact, which can often be quite a painful experience. But what we're hoping to find is something valuable. Something that isn't borrowed, but is truly unique.

Mining for gold

Childhood can be a fruitful source of inspiration for any writer, and those of us who write children's fiction ignore it at our peril. Some people seem to have almost total recall, whereas others

18

have – either consciously or unconsciously – banished it to some dark and dingy recess of their minds. Well, if you want to be a writer this is the time to blow away the cobwebs and take a closer look. Old family photographs can help; or talking to people who share your memories.

I wonder if you can recall being six, or eight, or ten. Do you remember the house you were living in then? The garden? The street? Who were the neighbours? Do you remember the school you went to? Who was your best friend? Did you really like them – or did they sometimes get up your nose? What was your relationship with your parents? Your place in the family, whether you were the oldest or the youngest or somewhere in the middle, may be significant. Or perhaps you were an only child, which can result in a quite different scenario.

Now try digging a little deeper. Can you remember something that happened, that made a lasting impression on you? It may have been a frightening experience, something you've never been able to forget, such as being locked in a cupboard or losing sight of your parents in a crowded street. Fear is a powerful *aide memoire*, but there will doubtless be other emotions you can recall, both positive and negative. The excitement of birthdays and Christmases; your first sight of the sea when you went on holiday, or of snow; the hero-worship you felt for an adult who was kind to you in that rather lordly way adults sometimes are; petty sibling jealousies; sudden friendships and equally sudden animosities; the shocking realisation that something or someone you trusted was not quite what they seemed to be.

Reading through this list you will almost certainly find at least one experience you recognise and can identify with. Indeed, you may find it a useful exercise to try writing it down as accurately as you possibly can. With luck you will be able to remember where you were and who you were with at the time, what you said and did and their reactions. You may even be able to take it a stage further and remember colours, smells, sounds. More importantly, you may remember how you *felt*, because emotion is the key that opens the magic box – and once you turn the key in the lock a host of potent memories come flooding back.

All very interesting, you may say, but what possible relevance can *my* childhood memories have when it comes to writing for

19

today's children? Obviously you can't take chunks of autobiographical material and try to pass it off as fiction – at least, not unless you are setting your story back in time and openly basing it on your own life. No, the object of this exercise is to put you in touch with the child you once were, to enable you to see things again through a child's eyes. Regard it, if you like, as a limbering-up exercise for what is to come. It may also provide you with a bonus in the shape of that vital spark, possibly something quite nebulous, which will get you started.

A whisper of a story

Of course that vital spark doesn't have to have come from your childhood. Throughout your life you will undoubtedly have had experiences that made an impression on you and simply demand to be used in some form or another. They may not even be deeply significant: sometimes a quite trivial incident will spark off an idea – a chance meeting, a story told by a stranger, a picture seen in an exhibition, music heard on the radio. Some writers are even inspired by a news item or a magazine article. All you need is that first mysterious "whisper of a story".

Fine. So what happens next?

Now this is where that strange alchemy, the magic that is the process of all creative writing, comes in. Because in my experience one idea is rarely enough: it has to await the time when a second comes along to "mate" with it and create new life. And the chances are that if one idea comes from outside yourself, eg from a newspaper cutting, the other idea will come from within. With luck it may even be ready and waiting. Or perhaps I should say *he* or *she* will be waiting, because the very best ideas often take the form of a character.

When I came to write *Only Miranda* I based the character of Miranda partly on myself and partly on a girl I was at school with. Miranda is an only child – hence the title – and she is fiercely independent, inventive and a bit of a crusader. She's also a rotten speller, loves poetry, hates sport but is an excellent swimmer – all characteristics of my old schoolfriend. But of course as soon as I started writing the book Miranda stopped being like either or us and became herself, because that is the way of fictional characters. They take on a life of their own; and by the time you've finished the book you probably won't even be able to remember who you based them on. Nonetheless they are far more likely to leap off the page as real, three-dimensional people than if you had simply conjured them out of thin air, which is a sure-fire recipe for creating stereotypes.

Writers are terrible thieves. We plunder not only our own lives but those of our family, friends and acquaintances, although with luck they won't be aware of our crime. Because what we do with our loot is to knock it about, remould it and transform it into something quite different – and, we hope, unrecognisable.

In other words, we add the personal touch.

Starting from where you are

Actually you don't have much choice. As a writer you can only start from where you are; and it makes no difference whether you're writing fantasy or ghost stories or crime, something of yourself is going to be present in that book. You may think you're invisible – you may even deliberately attempt to conceal your identity – but anyone who knows you well will be able to spot certain tell-tale clues. The person you are – your background, upbringing, life experiences, passions and prejudices – will inevitable colour everything you write. And that's how it should be, otherwise your writing will be bland and ordinary and dull.

We're constantly being told to "write about what we know". Taken too literally this can be very limiting, at least where fiction is concerned, but when it comes to the background of a story it certainly helps to have a working knowledge of what you're writing about. True, this can be researched, but somehow a researched background never quite has that ring of truth about it that comes from personal experience.

The beauty of this for a writer is that nothing that's ever happened to you need be wasted. You can draw on everything you've ever seen or done throughout the course of your life. If you've ever visited a foreign country – or better still, lived in one – make use of it as a setting for a story. If you've played a musical instrument, let one of your characters do the same. If you have a passion for sailing, send your fictional children off on a sailing holiday. I'm not saying you should *only* write about what you know, merely that if you can do so it helps.

You will also need to draw on personal experience when it comes to setting the scene, because if *you* can't imagine the place you're describing the chances are that the reader won't be able to either. Close your eyes for a moment and think of a location of which you have a particularly vivid recollection. It may be London or Venice; a seaside town or a country village; a river bank; a shopping centre; a ski resort; a swimming pool. Now, using all five of your senses, try to describe that scene in a way that will bring it alive to someone else. Sunlight on water; the honking of car horns; the taste of Italian ice-cream; the scrunch of snow beneath your feet; the pungent smell of chlorine. Just one or two telling phrases based on your personal recollections will be far more evocative than a long, boring paragraph of conventional description – the sort of thing that I, and probably most other readers, usually skip.

In other words, you're gathering material constantly, on all sorts of different levels. The important thing is that this material is personal to *you*. It's not somebody else's material, it's yours. Which means that the story that springs from it will be unique.

The next question is, what are you going to do with it?

Weaving new patterns

In her wonderful book, *Dear Writer*, Carmel Bird advises aspiring authors to "take the matter of their own existence and weave that matter into new patterns".

Sometimes, in a Creative Writing class, a student will produce a rather meandering short story, and if the tutor suggests it needs more shape and perhaps a different ending the student will say, "Ah, but that's exactly how it happened. It really did happen to me, you see." Well, yes, the tutor had probably already guessed. But using the raw material of our own lives is only the beginning.

The rest – and it's a substantial rest – is where the craft comes in. Now you have to make the raw material into a complete, well-crafted story.

As I'm sure you're aware, any trip into our own unconscious is fraught with potential danger. The greatest and most obvious is that we are seduced by what we find there, trapped and held captive. By this I mean that, like the student who tries to tell a story "as it really happened", it's so much easier to wallow around happily in our memories than to bring them to the surface, examine them in the clear light of day, extract what we want out of them, rearrange them and present them in an entirely different form. If you have read Dorothea Brande's classic *Becoming a Writer* you will be aware of the need to balance the inspiration you get from your unconscious with the shaping and editing skills of your conscious mind.

What you are aiming to achieve is the kind of truth that is only possible if your story springs from the right source. If you look at all the enduring classics, the ones that are as popular with children today as when they were written, you will see that they have in them some element that strikes a deeper chord. Even though their language may be dated, and some of the description too long or too ornate for today's tastes, nonetheless they have at their core something timeless. Something that still works, that has an appeal for today's children. It's a deeply personal thing, this communication between writer and reader. Personal and mysterious.

Mind you, when people ask "Where do you get your ideas from?" I'm still floored, because usually they want a simple answer and there's nothing simple about the matter of our existence. It's deep and complex and mysterious and infinitely exciting. You just don't know what's there till you start digging.

And when you've found your raw material the next stage is to start weaving it into the kind of story that will appeal to today's children.

4

CHARACTER AND VIEWPOINT

At a guess your original idea will have come in the form of a character or characters in a certain situation; or you may have thought of the situation first and put some characters into it. Either way, those characters are going to be the most important factor in your story and it is they who must engage your reader's interest. That's why it's worth spending a little time and trouble on getting to know them.

You may have noticed, by the way, that I've been careful to use the word "characters" rather than people, since in a children's book the central character may well be non-human. But it makes no difference whether your story revolves around a child, an animal, a robot, or a monster from outer space, we must still be able to believe in them.

Getting to know your characters

Sometimes, if you're lucky, characters will spring into your mind fully-formed, so full of vitality you can't wait to start writing about them. More often than not, however, they sneak up on you. They may be suggested by certain traits in yourself or in someone you know well; or by the appearance of someone you've met quite casually. After all, you're surrounded by characters everywhere you go. The more observant you are, the more overwhelmed you will be by the abundance of raw material.

Most fictional characters, even when based on real-life people, are an amalgam. You may take the quirk of an eyebrow from one, the infectious giggle from another, the tendency to embroider the truth from a third and the passion for loud music from a fourth. With luck the result will add up to a credible, well-rounded personality.

Next you need to get to know them inside out and how you do this depends entirely on your own preferences. It can be a purely mental exercise, in which you spend every available moment thinking about those characters until they begin to come alive. Or you may like to write down as many details about them as you can, such as date of birth, colour of hair, colour of eyes, favourite food, favourite TV programmes, etc. This background material gives them substance, even if you don't make use of it when it comes to writing the actual story, and will also help you to avoid making obvious mistakes, such as changing the colour of their eyes halfway through.

One word of warning, though. Don't get them so rigidly fixed in your mind that they have no room to breathe. Allowing characters to grow and change is what gives a book its dynamism. Sometimes they may even take you, their creator, by surprise and when that happens you know that miraculously they've acquired a life of their own. Now your only problem is to keep them under control!

Finding the right name

Sometimes a character will arrive in your head complete with name, physical appearance and personality. Once I had such a vivid dream about a famous female inventor called Dame Barbara Blanchflower that a whole story grew up around her – and when her arch-rival turned out to be Dr Lucius Delabole it seemed inconceivable that he could ever have been called anything else.

More often than not, however, you will end up poring over books of names designed for parents-to-be, which in a way is what you are. Because this is an absolutely vital stage in the creation of your book: give a character the wrong name and somehow the story won't work, but give them the right one and the rest will follow. Can you imagine if Paddington Bear had been called Euston? Or if Pippi Longstocking had been called Mary Shortsocks?

Surnames are equally important. If we're lazy we plump for the obvious, such as Smith or Clark or Johnson; but a browse through the local telephone directory may throw up something far more interesting, such as Spragg or Delaney or Brinkmeyer. They don't have to be long or outlandish to be memorable: what matters is that they fit the character.

One important point to remember is to vary the names that you choose, and if possible don't have them begin with the same letter. For example, if Richard and Robert appear in the same scene the reader will almost certainly get confused: likewise Sarah and Susan.

As well as the telephone directory, a useful source of surnames can be the lists supplied by various clubs and organisations; and when it comes to naming your fictional children a recent school list will give you the Christian names currently in fashion.

Physical description

There are three ways in which you can convey to your readers how your characters look and sound. The first is obvious: you can describe their appearance. But how much physical description do you need to give?

Clearly a complete run-down of height, colouring and body weight as each new character appears would be boring and unimaginative. Nonetheless you do need to convey some kind of visual image. The best way is to pick out one or two unusual features, such as a freckled nose or rimless spectacles, and mention them a couple of times early on to establish that image in the readers' minds. The rest of the detail they can fill in for themselves.

You can also convey a great deal by their actions. For example, if a man has to stoop as he enters the room, then you needn't state that he's tall. Actions, too, can tell us what kind of people they are. Rather than stating flatly, "Evadne loved getting others into trouble", it's far better to *show* us Evadne getting someone into trouble.

The third way of establishing a character is through dialogue. When we first meet someone our immediate impression is inevitably based on the way they look, but this may change completely as soon as we hear them speak. A character's voice, tone and manner of speaking is all part of their personality, and the reader can often learn more from a single speech than from several paragraphs of description.

Age and gender

Is it necessary to mention a character's age?

I must confess that my natural inclination is to be rather vague on the subject. Rather than state a character's age in black-and-white I usually try to convey it in more subtle ways, eg by referring to the year or grade they're in at school, or to their position in the family in relation to their older or younger siblings, and let readers draw their own conclusions. Otherwise you can end up with something that reads like a news item: Lucy, ten, met Debbie, nine-and-a-half, in the park ...

It's advisable to make your central character or characters slightly older than the readership you're aiming at. Children are very conscious of their position on the age scale, and if they suddenly discover that the boy or girl they're reading about is actually younger than themselves they are liable to lose interest and write the whole story off as "babyish".

When it comes to gender boys tend to prefer stories built around a central male character, whereas girls are more likely to be more open-minded. A lot depends, of course, on the age group you're writing for. Very young children are blessedly non-sexist, but as they grow older the gender gap inevitably widens, so that if you're writing for the over-tens the chances are you will have to make a conscious decision, something most writers do very reluctantly.

There are various ways of achieving equal boy/girl appeal. The most obvious is to make the central character non-human and therefore acceptable to both sexes: or you can have two main characters, one of each sex, and try to keep the narrative balance fairly even. However, there are certain genres which seem able to cross the great divide, such as fantasy, horror and science fiction, perhaps because they are so far removed from most children's everyday experience as to make the question irrelevant.

Rounded personalities

How can you make your characters three-dimensional?

If you're writing a realistic story there's no place for the all-good hero or the all-bad villain: they belong to the realm of myth and fairy-tale. Far more interesting is the hero who has a tendency to distort the truth; or the villain who is devoted to his dog. The paradox, the unexpected trait, is what will give your character depth. If you have a child as the central character take care you don't make him a cardboard cut-out to whom things happen while leaving him basically unaffected. Your hero and/or heroine must be *doers*, active participants in the plot, with faults as well as virtues. But of course, if you're writing from inside the character and not as the detached storyteller, this won't be a danger.

Don't be afraid to make your subsidiary characters slightly – or even outrageously – larger than life. They should be entertaining and memorable, not mere tools of the plot. Often it's these secondary characters that leave the most lasting impression – look at Mr Toad in *The Wind in the Willows* – so it's well worth putting a little extra effort into their creation rather than sketching them in with a few perfunctory strokes.

Parents can be a particular hazard. It's all too easy to settle for the old bland stereotype, the cosy Mums and dependable Dads who used to hover in the background of the storybooks we read in our youth. These days writers have a different approach, allowing their adult characters to be as quirky and unreliable as they can be in real life. To my mind, this has the effect of making them more likeable as well as more believable. To depict parents, teachers and adults-in-general as faceless authoritarian cyphers is doing no one a service, least of all the children you're writing for.

Beware too of that sweet old white-haired granny in a rocking-chair! Today's grandparents are more likely to be into aerobics or amateur dramatics.

Whose viewpoint?

Possibly the most vital decision you have to make is through whose eyes you are going to tell the story. Children have an amazing ability to lose themselves so completely in a story that they become totally involved with the central character. Indeed, for the period of time during which they are reading or listening to a story they *are* that character, and for this reason it's important to avoid any sudden lapses or changes of viewpoint which will break their concentration.

You have, broadly speaking, three options:

1. Omniscient viewpoint
This is sometimes known as "author talking" or a "God's eye" viewpoint. In other words, the story is being told in a detached, impersonal manner and not as experienced by any one character. For example:

> It was a wild and windy night and the boats were tugging restlessly at their moorings. At one end of the harbour stood a rough stone cottage, and from an upstairs window a light flashed intermittently, sending its message out to sea.

This is a perfectly valid style of storytelling, very popular in 19th century fiction, but not really to be recommended when writing for children. There are times when you may find it useful, for example if you're writing a mystery or ghost story and want to set up an intriguing situation before the story properly begins. However, as a narrative device it has its pitfalls and you need to be aware of them.

2. Third person viewpoint
This is by far the most commonly used form of narrative. It enables you, while maintaining your role as storyteller, to get inside the skin of one – or possibly more – of your characters, so that the reader can share the thoughts and feelings of that character and thus feel directly involved.

I say "possibly more", but when writing for children it's advisable to limit your viewpoint characters to two or three at the most. In fact, unless it's absolutely necessary, it's safer to limit yourself to one viewpoint only. This way you are far more likely to hold your reader's interest throughout. Certainly younger children find it very difficult to take an imaginative leap out of one character, with whom they have already begun to identify, into another.

By far the most confusing thing you can do is to change viewpoints within the same scene. This causes that sudden jolt and break of concentration that I mentioned earlier. Here is an example:

> Sarah snatched the book out of Pete's hands and held it to her chest.
> "You're not to look at it," she said fiercely. "It's private."
> Pete wondered what she was making all the fuss about. Just a load of old poems, that's all it was, written in Sarah's round, childish hand. Nothing significant.
> Sarah turned away to hide her hot, embarrassed face.

To be suddenly thrust into Pete's mind, even for one brief paragraph, not only undermines the reader's sense of identification with Sarah, but strikes a false note. In real life we never know what the other person is thinking and that's why human relationships can be so difficult and so full of mystery. Rewritten from Sarah's viewpoint only, that scene would read like this:

> Sarah snatched the book out of Pete's hands and held it to her chest.
> "You're not to look at it," she said fiercely. "It's private."
> Pete stared at her. She could see he was wondering why on earth she was making such a fuss about a poetry book and turned away to hide her hot, embarrassed face.

3. First person viewpoint

Stories told in the first person have many advantages and some disadvantages. The main advantage is a high level of reader involvement: everything that happens is seen through one character's eyes and the readers know exactly what's going on inside his head. You are, of course, limited strictly to that one viewpoint: however this limitation can be converted into a strength, as we've seen.

Perhaps the main difficulty to overcome is the awkwardness with which your viewpoint character must speak of himself. For example, if he sounds too self-congratulatory he may come across as big-headed. You also have to guard against too much introspection.

So how do you decide whether to tell your story in the first person or the third?

Usually your decision is dictated by the type of story you want to write, but if you have any doubts it may be a good idea to try it out both ways. For example, I was experimenting recently with the opening of a story for young adults. It concerns a girl who wants to leave school early, against the advice of her teachers and friends, so that she can stay at home and housekeep for her beloved but disorganised father – a highly unfashionable ambition. My first attempt went something like this:

> Pippa climbed the hill behind Monkswood and stood with her back against a beech tree, gazing down at the house she loved. She knew every stick and stone of it. It was her home. And tomorrow she would be leaving school for good ...

Boring, isn't it? Just like every other book you've ever read – and there must be dozens – which start with the heroine on top of a hill, gazing fondly down at the dear old homestead.

So I tried putting it into the first person. Taking me by surprise, it came out like this:

> On the day I left school for good I thought that all my worries were over. How wrong can you be?

Obviously this is the opening of a completely different book. No more sentimental mooning about on hilltops. This heroine will be far more down to earth.

To sum up, you need:

1. To know your characters inside out;
2. To find exactly the right names for them;
3. To make them rounded rather than flat stereotypes;
4. To convey clearly how they look, act and sound;
5. To decide through whose viewpoint you are going to tell the story.

31

5

GETTING STARTED

What should you do when that vital spark, that mysterious "whisper of a story" first comes to you?

Well, if you're a highly organised person you probably reach for your notebook and write it down quickly before you forget it. On the other hand, you may prefer to leave it alone for a while and let it take its chance. My own feeling is that if an idea is strong and significant enough to form the basis of a book, then it is in no danger of allowing itself to be forgotten. It will keep coming back again and again, battering against the door of your consciousness and demanding to be written.

However, the way you choose to work will largely be dictated by the sort of person you are. There is no right or wrong way of doing things, only the way that suits *you*, and if you feel happier keeping an "ideas" book, then that's what you should do.

Most writers would agree, I think, that an idea needs a period of gestation. It is during this "growing" stage that you can look at it from all angles, size up its potential and decide how best to put it to work. This is also when it can be helpful to think about the underlying theme. For example, is your picture story about a lost teddy bear really about a child seeking love? Or your novel about a teenage girl taking up hang-gliding really about her search for an identity? If you know in advance this may save you making a few false starts, or taking a wrong turning with the plot. But if you haven't a clue, don't worry. Very often the theme doesn't become clear until you start writing.

Pre-planning

How much pre-planning should you do?

Again, this is entirely up to you. You may find it helpful to write down a list of chapter numbers or headings on one side of a sheet of paper and set against them a rough outline of what is going to happen in each one. Some writers go further than this, working out time charts and planning in detail the contents of each chapter before they are ready to start. Clearly this is a matter of temperament. Most writers, when they begin, have at least a vague idea where they are going but may not be too sure how they're going to get there. They prefer to leave themselves free to alter course if something interesting crops up to take them off in a new direction. This makes the writing of a book an exciting, even dangerous, voyage of discovery.

However, if you are lucky enough to be commissioned to write a book, the publisher will need a synopsis before he can offer a contract. He may also ask to see the first chapter. Now, this first chapter is all-important. It sets the scene, establishes the characters, and provides the impetus to get the story under way. My own experience is that if I write the synopsis first it may well kill the story stone dead; but once Chapter One is written everything becomes much easier. I have "caught" the characters on paper and the book has already taken off. Now I can write the synopsis because I have a much better idea of how the story is likely to turn out.

This business of synopsis-writing can be a real bugbear. My advice is to keep it as brief as possible, preferably no more than a page and a half, and try to convey the feeling and atmosphere of the story rather than describe every twist and turn of the plot. An over-long, over-detailed synopsis can swiftly put a publisher off the whole idea. Much better to send him something short and punchy, more in the nature of a "blurb", that will make him think here is a book he *must* have on his autumn list.

Incidentally, if when you start writing you find you want to deviate slightly from your original synopsis, don't worry. No publisher will object to changes that result in a better finished product.

Now let's take a look at that all-important first chapter.

Where should the story begin?

This is not such a foolish question as it sounds. The most common fault among novice writers is to begin a book too far back, or alternatively to plunge their readers headlong into confusion by failing to set the scene adequately first. And remember, when you are writing for children clarity is vital, especially at the beginning. If a child is confused he is far less likely to persist with a story than an adult. So you must catch his interest as quickly as possible, and hold it by involving him in a situation he finds intriguing.

An excellent piece of advice about the right place to start was given to me by Dianne Doubtfire, whose book *The Craft of Novel-writing* is a companion volume in this series. "A good place to begin a story," she said, "is just before a change takes place in the life of your central character."

How many books have you read which open with a journey to a new location? Or the arrival of a visitor to shatter hitherto peaceful lives? Or a sudden alteration in family fortunes, usually for the worse? All these openings involve some sort of change which will pitchfork the central character into a situation of conflict.

When George, in C. Day Lewis's children's classic *The Otterbury Incident*, is wondering where to begin, his English teacher tells him to "jump right into the deep end of the story, don't hang about on the edge." In other words, it's a good idea to open with a big scene, something dramatic that will grab your reader's attention and hold it long enough for you to get the characters established.

Finding the right voice

Finding the right "voice" is essential: it sets the tone for the rest of the book and gives it that stamp of individuality which makes it different from any other. No matter whether you're writing in the first or third person, your opening paragraphs will signal to your readers what kind of a book this is going to be. Take, for example, the opening of my children's novel, *Message from Venus*:

"Now close your eyes," Ma said, "and let your minds go blank." My mind was already blank. It couldn't have been much blanker. We – that is my mother, my older sister Aisling and me – sat round the kitchen table with the Lexicon cards arranged in a circle and our fingertips resting on an upturned wineglass. We were not playing games. Quite seriously, we were trying to find out where my father had gone.

By now – I hope! – my readers will know roughly what to expect and can settle down in the appropriate frame of mind.

This underlines the need to be consistent. Once you have started your story using a certain voice then you must stick to it. It would be unforgivable to open in a bright and breezy fashion and then switch to stark melodrama halfway through. Your readers would feel they had been let down.

The question of "voice" is of course bound up with style, but they are not quite the same thing. Your style is you, and – provided you are writing naturally and not trying to copy other people – will colour everything you do. It is far more subtle and deep-rooted than the "voice" which can, and should, be different for every book. An actor may be convincing in many different roles, but to each he brings that special quality which is his own unique style.

Establishing your characters

Try not to introduce too many characters in the first chapter or the reader will become confused. You know what it's like when you arrive at a party and your hostess insists on telling you every-one's name as soon as you enter the room. You can't possibly take in more than a few, and won't be able to put names to faces until you actually engage in conversation with them. Who is your view-point character? Let's stay with him, get to know what he's thinking and what sort of person he is. Then you can introduce the other characters gradually as they enter the story.

If possible it's best to avoid mentioning a character before they actually make their first appearance. Sometimes you may need to do this for a reason, perhaps to build up the reader's expectations by dropping hints or even threats about what to expect when this character finally appears. But if there isn't a dramatic reason for doing so it's best not to describe them in any detail too early, or the reader will have difficulty keeping the information in his head before he has a peg to hang it on.

Setting the scene

Setting the scene is not merely a question of describing the geographical location where your story is to take place, but embraces the whole tricky business of conveying to the reader, as unobtrusively as possible, a wealth of information about the imaginary world he is about to enter. The keyword here is "unobtrusively". Nothing is more offputting to your readers than to be faced with three or four pages of facts about the central character's past life before the story properly begins. Yet those facts may be vital to their understanding. So how do you get them over?

Here's how NOT to do it:

Daisy lived with her father and mother in a small house on the outskirts of the town. She loved animals and longed for a pet, but her mother refused to let her have a cat or a dog. Daisy thought this was unfair. After all, her father kept pigeons. But her mother said that was all right because he kept them outside in the yard where it didn't matter if they made a mess. It was having animals indoors that she objected to. So Daisy began to make a secret plan.

Not exactly an original opening, or a very arresting one. "A small house on the outskirts of the town" tells us absolutely nothing about the place that Daisy lives, nor do we get a clear picture of her or her parents as characters. The only good thing about it is that we now know what it is that Daisy wants – a pet – and we might even be intrigued by the idea that she has a secret plan. But this information could have been conveyed in a far more interesting and enlightening way. For example:

36

Daisy rested her chin on her hands and gazed through the kitchen window into the backyard. Dad was talking to his pigeons again, gently stroking their greeny-grey feathers and telling them how beautiful they were. Every day when he got home from work he hardly bothered to say hello to her or Mum, but went straight out into the yard to see his beloved birds.

She sighed. "Mum, please can I have a – ?"

"No, Daisy," Mum said firmly. "It's out of the question. This house is cramped enough as it is."

"But it's not fair. Dad has his pigeons, so why can't I – "

"I said *no*, Daisy!"

Here the scene-setting takes the form of action combined with dialogue. We know that Dad is gentle and Mum is firm, and can draw our own conclusions as to what the relationship between them is like. We also know that the house is small, because Mum has said that it's cramped. And we know that Daisy wants something, although we may not yet be quite certain what it is. But no matter, that can come later. No need to rush things at this stage. The rest can be filtered in once you've got the story under way.

The first chapter

Writing that vital first chapter will tell you a lot about the story as a whole, especially as regards the overall shape of the book. It will almost certainly find its own length, and this will give you a good indication of how long the rest of the chapters should be. You will also have established your characters, set the scene and got the plot under way. Be warned, you had better be prepared to alter it several times, because it's very unlikely you will have got it right first time. But should you spend time on getting it right *now* or wait until you have finished the book?

Here we have to come back to methods of working and how important it is for you to find what's best for you. Some people like to correct and polish as they go along; others prefer to wait until they get to the end. I myself fall into the second category, mainly because I find it impossible to revise what I have written until the story is finished and I can see the shape of it. In other words, I belong to the bash-on-regardless school of writing. However this means that when I start revising I often find that my opening chapter has to be virtually rewritten in the light of what is to come.

Either way, it's worth taking time and trouble over getting it right. Of course you may be lucky and get it perfect first time, but if your instinct tells you that it could be better, then don't begrudge the extra effort it may cost. It may well be the best investment you will ever make.

To sum up:

1. Give yourself plenty of "thinking time".
2. Find the right "voice" for your viewpoint character.
3. Begin with a dramatic scene to grab your reader's attention.
4. Don't introduce too many characters at once.
5. Filter in your background information gradually.

6

BRINGING YOUR STORY TO LIFE

When you write a story you are creating a make-believe world in which a set of imaginary characters play their part in a drama you have invented for them. Yet, if you want to hold your readers' interest, you must convince them that all this is actually happening, that it's as real as the world they inhabit, and that the fate of these characters is important.

So how do you bring your story to life?

Motivation and conflict

Quite near the beginning, preferably on the first page, you need to have established what your central character's problem is.

But surely, you may say, it's not essential for the central character to have a problem, not in a children's book? Well, unless at least one of your characters *wants* something, and unless they have to overcome some kind of obstacle that stands between them and the object of their desire, you don't really have a story. That is, of course, a piece of gross oversimplification. Nonetheless, a story in which the central character sails through situations with no difficulties at all will inevitably lack both depth and interest.

Conflict is the stuff of which fiction is made. This doesn't mean, of course, that your characters have to be constantly arguing with each other. That would be tedious. But conflict can take many different forms – the insecurity felt by a small child on moving house; the dangers encountered by an urban fox in his hunt for food; the hostility of parents towards a teenager's new and – in their eyes – undesirable friend. What your readers will want to know is how your characters are going to deal with the situation in which they find themselves. Probably not too well at first; but gradually, though trial and error, they will succeed. It's the "trial and error" that makes the story: if they succeed first time there's no suspense.

Thoughts and feelings

The secret of drawing your readers into the story is to allow them to share in the thoughts and feelings of your central character. It's no use describing a spooky scene in a haunted house without letting us know that your hero is scared stiff – because if he's not scared your readers won't be either. And if your heroine is having a tussle with her conscience – should she go to the party without her parents' permission? – we need to know exactly how she arrives at her decision, whatever it may be, so that we can understand and sympathise.

In other words, you have to get right inside your character, not only seeing everything from her viewpoint but also feeling whatever emotions she may be feeling as well. This applies to all age groups and all kinds of stories. It's only when that lost teddy bear becomes worried about his predicament and longs to be reunited with his owner that your young reader will start to *care* about his fate.

This also applies when it comes to setting the scene. Clearly description *for its own sake* is always a mistake. It is a great temptation, especially when describing a location you know well, to let yourself go with a piece of stunningly poetic prose, but the danger is that this will turn out to be a blatant case of "author talking". In other words, you've momentarily stepped outside your viewpoint character to give us an impersonal description of a landscape, which means about as much as a picture postcard sent from abroad. As soon as you step back inside your character than we get an entirely different view, since we're seeing it through *his* eyes and therefore experiencing *his* emotional reactions to the scene. Perhaps he finds the landscape beautiful but oppressive; the busyness of a city street may underline his loneliness; or the dark, still waters of a lake suggest menace. In other words, if every piece of description is directly related to the mood and emotions of your viewpoint character, there is no risk of it being superfluous to the plot.

Making a scene of it

These days we are all – adults as well as children – used to watching a great deal of drama on television, whether in the form of crime series, old films, or soap opera. As a result many writers tend to think quite naturally in terms of "scenes", which means that their stories make a strong impact on young readers already conditioned to expect this kind of treatment. Dramatisation is sometimes called the hidden art of storytelling. As readers, you may be unaware of the reason why a story fails to grab you: you only know that a piece of narrative has been going on for pages and nothing seems to have happened. In fact a lot may have happened, but because it hasn't been dramatised you've missed it.

Here are two ways of dealing with the same incident:

First example:
When they reached the wood Mark hung back. "What's the matter?" Susie demanded. "You're not scared, are you?"

"Of course not." He was stung by the scorn in her voice. "It's just that it looks – well, a bit sinister."

"How can it be sinister? It's only a wood, for heaven's sake." Impatiently Susie strode ahead and disappeared into the trees.

After a few moments Mark followed, although his heart was beating fast. At once the trees seemed to close in on him, whispering to each other as he passed between them. He could hear Susie moving through the undergrowth and tried hard to catch up, but somehow she eluded him. At last he stood still and when he had caught his breath he called out, "Susie? Sue, where are you?"

There was no answer. Nor could he any longer hear sounds of movement. Everything seemed deathly quiet, as if he were completely alone.

Second example:

As soon as they reached the wood Mark hung back. When Susie demanded why, he told her that the wood seemed to him sinister, but she only laughed and strode ahead, disappearing among the trees. After a moment Mark followed, trying hard to catch up; but somehow she eluded him. At last he stood still and called her name, but she didn't answer. He seemed to be completely alone.

The same incident, but I hope you will agree with me that the first version is far more likely to appeal to a young reader than the second. This is because it has been dramatised. Instead of telling the story as a straight piece of narration I've "made a scene of it".

Remember, though, that each scene must have a purpose, either to further the story or to tell us something significant about the characters. Beautifully written, true-to-life vignettes are fine for soap opera because the stories are open-ended; but a novel must have shape and structure and be heading for a satisfying conclusion.

Dialogue

Children love plenty of conversation in a story. Not only does it help to bring the characters to life, but it also looks interesting on the page, breaking up those wearisome chunks of prose. Again, though, it must be there for a purpose: aimless chit-chat that doesn't lead anywhere will only bore the reader.

The trouble is, of course, that real-life conversations tend to be about ninety-per-cent chit-chat. But, if you listen hard, you'll realise that amidst all that verbiage about the shocking weather we've been having lately and the chronic state of Aunt Ethel's health are hidden some vital nuggets of information. It's the writer's task to select those nuggets and discard everything that is superfluous. In other words, what may appear on the printed page as natural conversation is in fact nothing of the sort. It is only the writer's skill that creates an illusion of spontaneity.

It helps if you have an ear for the rhythms and cadences of

everyday speech. If you haven't, then you may have to work a little harder, being constantly on your guard against putting stilted, contrived remarks into your character's mouth. A good test is to read aloud what you have written and ask yourself, Does it *sound* right? Better still, put it on to a cassette recorder so that you can listen to it more objectively.

Remember, you can control the pace and mood of a scene by the use of dialogue. Obviously a short, sharp interchange between two characters will convey speed and urgency, whereas a long soliloquy slows the pace right down and suggests a dreamy, intro-spective mood. On the whole, it's best to keep speeches fairly short when writing for children. If a character does hold forth for any length of time then the subject matter must be so rivetting there's no danger of your reader's interest being lost.

As far as possible, try to avoid setting your dialogue within the framework of a static situation. Children, being naturally active creatures, tend to talk on the move, so it's far more convincing to have them exchanging remarks while scaling a wall or fishing for tadpoles in a pond. This helps to keep things lively, as well as establishing a strong visual image for the reader to hold in his mind while the dialogue is taking place. Also, in a book for younger children, where there are line drawings on nearly every page, it will give the illustrator plenty of scope.

When writing dialogue there are certain accepted conventions which it may be useful to summarize:

1. Always start a new paragraph when you have a change of speaker. If a character makes two consecutive speeches, inter-rupted by action, they can both be contained within the same paragraph.

   Example:
   "Look what I've found." Ralph opened the box to reveal a curiously shaped stone studded with tiny fragments of shell. "What do you think it is?"

2. Stylistically it is preferable to use "he said, she said" than to introduce too many variations such as gasped, cried, expostu-lated, remonstrated etc. In fact, as readers, we are so used to

"he said, she said" that we hardly notice it, however repetitious its use, whereas the introduction of a more unusual verb of speech can be obtrusive. If you do use a variation make sure it justifies its existence by conveying the speaker's manner or tone of voice, rather than being there merely to ring the changes.

3. If you describe a character's actions when he's speaking then you don't need a verb of speech at all. Look again at the example in (1) above. I didn't bother to put "said Ralph" after the first speech because when Ralph went on to open the box it was obvious that it was he who had spoken.

4. If you have only two characters in a scene there is no need to identify them after every speech; the fact that you've started a new paragraph will tell your reader that there has been a change of speaker. You must, of course, establish at the beginning which of them speaks first; and every now and again the reader will need reminding of the speaker's identity just in case they've lost track. Younger children, especially, could easily be confused by a long sequence of unidentified speech. Ideally we should be able to tell who's who by the way they speak and the things they say, but if the speeches are short that's not always possible.

5. Everyday speech is most commonly characterised by the use of shortened forms, such as we'll, she'd, they've, etc. If used in full they tend to add emphasis, as in "We shall be there, I promise," or suggests that the character isn't speaking in his native tongue. This can of course be turned to your advantage if you want to convey that he's speaking rather formal English, with perhaps a slight accent, and is certainly preferable to trying to reproduce his speech phonetically.

6. By the same token, it's best to keep the use of dialect to a minimum. If you have a good ear you can convey regional differences in speech by careful choice of vocabulary and the way you structure a sentence. Such devices as phonetic spelling and the use of apostrophes to indicate dropped aitches are irritating and, to a child, often incomprehensible. If your story is

set in Scotland, for example, it is far better to try to capture the lilt and flavour of the Scottish tongue rather than make your characters express themselves solely in "Scots, wha hae"-type language, which is tedious to read and not particularly convincing.

7. Dialogue in historical novels can present a problem. Obviously you want to avoid relapsing into the odds-boddikins-stap-me-vitals school of language. But should you try as far as possible to reproduce the authentic speech of the period, or is it safer to settle for contemporary, idiomatic English? Somewhere between the two is probably the best answer. It would be a near-impossibility to reproduce authentic Anglo-Saxon, for example. Far better to write dialogue that sounds natural to modern ears, while avoiding the use of jarring anachronisms. Remember, nothing must get in the way of your readers' enjoyment, whether it is archaic dialogue they can't follow or a glaringly obtrusive piece of modern slang.

8. Unspoken thoughts can be set out in a number of ways, but the most commonly used convention is to begin with a capital letter and omit the quotation marks.

Example:
Harry thought, It's a good thing I burned that letter.

It is worth remembering that dialogue will constitute at least a third – possibly more – of your story. Not only does it fulfil the obvious function of furthering the plot, but it can also set the scene, convey a mood, express emotion, or describe action. Above all, it gives your narrative a quality of immediacy. Its importance, therefore, cannot be over-emphasised.

The worst sin

To my mind, the worst sin you can commit when writing for children is to be dull. Most children's writers, while hoping their work will inform and enlighten, know that it is unlikely to achieve either of these objectives, unless it manages at the same time to be entertaining. On the whole children have a fairly low threshold of boredom, so any tendency to stodginess should be sharply knocked on the head.

Children love to try and unravel mysteries. They love to test out their courage by being a little bit scared. Above all, they love to laugh. If you can introduce humour – natural, not forced – into your stories then you are off to a flying start. Be warned, though, that anything too subtle will go down like a lead balloon. What really appeals to them is pure slapstick, or an element of farce that contains more than a hint of the subversive. Funny, descriptive names help to make a story memorable. How about the Whipple-Scrumptious Fudgemallow Delight or Cavity-filling Caramels in Roald Dahl's *Charlie and the Chocolate Factory*?

But humour needn't be restricted solely to the more frivolous, lighthearted sort of book. When used skilfully in the treatment of even the most serious subjects it can often restore that sense of balance so important when you are writing for children.

To sum up, you can bring your story to life by:

1. Plenty of conflict.
2. Thoughts and feelings.
3. Making a scene of it.
4. Lively, natural-sounding dialogue.
5. Use of humour.

7

KEEP IT BUBBLING

Storytelling is an ancient art. The best of the storytellers, like Homer and Queen Scheherazade, knew exactly how to keep their listeners on the edge of their seats. Indeed, Scheherazade's life depended on her ability to do just that. Skilful construction, the spacing out of climaxes, and knowing exactly the point where you should leave your readers wanting to know what happens next – these are the techniques we shall be examining in this chapter.

Construction

When writing for children it is vital to keep the forward thrust of a story going all the time so that your readers feel they're being carried relentlessly onward. If you have ever tried reading aloud to a class of eight-year-olds you will be familiar with that subtle change in the atmosphere, an onset of restlessness, which occurs when a story temporarily loses its way. Perhaps the writer has indulged himself with a few paragraphs of beautifully written but unnecessary description. Or he may have sent his characters on a brief detour which appears to have nothing to do with the plot. Or maybe he has introduced a character who is just plain boring. Whatever the reason, the tension has been lost – and so has the audience.

Take care to space out your high points so that they build up the suspense. If you have a long stretch without much happening then perhaps you need to condense that section, or alternatively introduce some kind of conflict. If you find you have a scene without any conflict at all – even internal – then it's probably best left out altogether. Above all, there must always be a sense of something coming, an interesting development lurking just around the corner. There's a good old show-business maxim: Make 'em laugh, make 'em cry, make 'em *wait*. Any writer who bears that in mind can't go far wrong.

Although the transition between scenes should be as smooth as possible, you don't need to walk your characters through every minute of their day. If, for example, you are moving them from one location to another, there's no point in giving an account of their train journey, taxi-ride, or whatever, unless that journey is in itself significant and a vital part of the story. A single sentence is often enough to serve as a bridge from one scene to the next; or you can leave a double space to indicate a change of scene, mood or even viewpoint. This is a convention readers soon learn to accept, enabling you to move the story on swiftly without the need for tedious bridging passages.

There are many ways in which a writer can indicate the passing of time. The simplest are often the best, such as "next day" or "on the following day" or "later that morning" – although a cliché to be avoided at all costs is "The day of the fete dawned bright and clear". Incidentally, it's as well to keep track of your time scale. I recently wrote a story about some children going away for a week's holiday and halfway through I realised that I had completely lost count of how many days and nights had passed. In fact they were only four days into their holiday and I was nearly at the end of the story!

Chapter lengths

To say that a story will find its own length, and provide its own clues as to how best it may be constructed, may sound like wishful thinking: nonetheless it usually turns out that way.

Much depends, of course, on the type of story you are writing – and it's essential, before you begin, to have at least a vague idea what that is. I say "a vague idea", because a novice writer often doesn't know what kind of a story they are writing until they've written it. Fair enough. The important thing when you start is just to get something down on paper: you can worry later about where it's likely to fit into the market.

When you become more experienced, however, you will have a far clearer idea exactly what it is you're trying to do and this will inevitably impose some kind of a shape on your work. In later chapters I will be dealing with the various types of books in more detail, but for the time being it's enough to point out that most stories for younger children are between 1000 and 7,500 words in length. A novel for older children is usually between 12,000 and 35,000 words, and some are even longer. However publishers are becoming less and less keen to take risks on lengthy one-off novels by unknown writers, so it's advisable to keep your first effort fairly short rather than attempt something on an epic scale.

Writing your first chapter will tell you a great deal. Where does it naturally end? If you are writing for younger children you'll want to keep the structure fairly simple, perhaps dealing with only one scene. That's fine, because children like short chapters. Coming to the end of something gives them a sense of achievement. And does it end on a high note or with a question mark that will make them want to carry on reading? If the answer's yes then you've probably got it right. What's more, that first chapter will have established the pattern for the rest of the book.

Does this mean that all your chapters have to be the same length? Roughly, yes, although there are no hard and fast rules. You may find you have a short but vitally important scene which won't join on comfortably either to the preceding or to the following chapter. In that case it may be more telling if it's isolated. But remember, children like patterns. They need to know where they are with a book, so if you take them by surprise too often they may become irritated and give up altogether.

Avoiding contrivances

Wherever possible try to avoid contrivances. By that I mean devices that are introduced for the purpose of the story but which don't ring true. In fact this can't happen if you've got inside the skin of your characters, because they will dictate the course of the plot and make it impossible for you to force them into unnatural situations.

Unfortunately coincidences, which occur remarkably often in real life, always seem suspiciously convenient if you put them into a book. Whilst you may be able to get away with using one at the very beginning, so that it acts as the springboard of a plot, to introduce one at a later point will look remarkably like contrivance.

Flashbacks are not a good idea, especially in a children's story. It's often tempting to use one at the beginning of a story in order to establish what has gone before, but it's far better to feed the information in gradually, perhaps through conversation, rather than break the forward flow of the narrative.

By far the worst kind of contrivance, though, is what I call "bringing in the US cavalry". In other words, to resolve the plot by introducing a completely new and unrelated factor at the last moment, merely for the sake of convenience. This can take the form of parents-to-the-rescue, instead of letting your child characters get themselves out of trouble, or the good-heavens-he-isn't-dead-after-all type solution to a mystery. Either way your readers will feel cheated.

Saggy middles

Sometimes, I must warn you, there's a period around the middle of the book when you begin to wonder if you have lost control. In my own mind I term this "middle-aged spread". It happens when the threads running through your story are beginning to proliferate and there's a danger that the pattern you're weaving is losing its shape. I don't know how other writers deal with this, but I suspect they all have different methods. My own is to forge on, trying to keep hold of the most important threads, until eventually I find my way out of the labyrinth. Later, when the book is finished, I'll go back to that middle section and re-work it in the light of subsequent development. This is because I find it difficult to see the book as a whole until the final chapter is written. Only then do I have a clear picture of what its shape should be.

Other writers may work quite differently, preferring to get it right before they go any further, and those who have carefully pre-planned their work probably don't have this problem at all. So once again you'll have to find the method that best accords with your own temperament. Whichever way you work, however, be prepared to make several drafts of each chapter, if necessary, until you are satisfied with what you've done.

As a rough guide, in a book of – say – fifteen chapters, you need to start building towards the climax somewhere around Chapter Twelve, so that what evolves from that point onwards slowly gathers momentum, sweeping characters and readers alike towards the final glorious conclusion.

Some common pitfalls

There are a lot of pitfalls awaiting the unwary writer and we all fall into them from time to time. If your story isn't working – or even if it's going like a bomb and you can't see anything wrong with it – watch out for the following:

1. Lack of pace. This can be due to too much introspection, where the character keeps stopping to tell us what he's thinking. There may be long stretches without any action; or some scenes may go on too long without having much content.

2. Lack of suspense. Whatever kind of story you are writing you need to drop little clues quite early on about what is likely to happen later in the story. Is that strange woman lurking around on the river bank something to do with the ghostly noises heard at night – or is there a perfectly rational explanation for her presence as everyone seems to think? Make your readers ask questions. Sow seeds of suspicion in their minds and keep them well watered as the story progresses.

3. Too many characters. An over-populated story is a sure way of losing your grip on the reader's interest. Generally speaking, the shorter the story the less characters you need – and every one of them must be made to work for their living. It may be

that dotty Aunt Mabel is superfluous to the plot; or perhaps you can condense two of the heroine's schoolfriends into one.

4. Not enough sparkiness. Any sparkiness going is usually generated by the characters, so perhaps they need livening up a bit? Maybe they are just too ordinary. Or it could be your prose style that's at fault. Check that it isn't becoming too ponderous and pedestrian.

5. A tendency to preachiness. This is usually caused by failure to get right inside your viewpoint character. As long as you maintain a measure of adult detachment you're in danger of making moral judgements that sound a false note and may well alienate your young readers.

6. Self-indulgence. Have you allowed yourself to becoming expansive on your favourite subject? If using a specific location have you waxed lyrical about its scenic delights at the expense of the plot? Have you written a passage of brilliantly witty dialogue which has nothing to do with the story? Then I'm afraid it's time to "murder your darlings". Yes, I know it hurts, but the end result will be all the better for it.

The final chapter

An editor once said to me that the closing chapter of a children's book should be like the grand finale of a pantomime – everyone assembled on stage, revealed at last in their true colours, to take their farewell bow. It depends, of course, on the type of book you're writing, but certainly there should be some kind of grand climax, a drawing together of threads, that will send your audience away feeling they've had their money's worth.

Drawing up the threads, however, and tying them in a satisfying knot, can be a tricky business. What you must avoid at all costs is a scene akin to the denouement in the old-style detective novel, where the Inspector gathers together all the suspects in the drawing-room and holds forth for several pages about who did what and why. Ideally, the reader should have been made aware as the story unfolded exactly why the characters acted as they did, so that by the time you reach the final chapter there's no need to analyse everyone's motives. Action, not explanation, is what children are hoping for at the end of a story – the grand bust-up, with the hero triumphant and the villain getting his come-uppance.

For older readers this can be done with more subtlety. It is possible, even desirable, to leave at least one thread untied, one question unanswered, so that they can draw their own conclusions. The reaction that you, as the writer, are hoping for is the long drawn-out sigh of satisfaction. Of course, that's how it had to end! But at the same time you want the reader to feel that the characters will go on with their lives after the book is closed.

Be careful, too, that you finish immediately you have nothing important left to say. Once, to my shame, an editor had to cut the final two paragraphs of my book because I'd let it drag on beyond its natural conclusion. Rather like seeing someone off at a railway station, if the train doesn't move out on time your smile becomes fixed and your waves mechanical.

So when you come to the end – stop.

To sum up:

1. Let your first chapter establish the pattern.
2. Space out the high points.
3. Avoid contrivances.
4. End each chapter on a high note, or with a question mark.
5. End the story with action, not explanation.

8

PICTURE BOOKS (0-7)

Babies Need Books is the title of Dorothy Butler's comprehensive study, based on her belief that "books can be used not only to entertain and to comfort, but also to stimulate the imagination, to stir the emotions and to help the early forging of relationships". Children who have access to books at an early age are likely to regard them as friends and companions for the rest of their lives; whereas children deprived of books may well see them as alien tools, even instruments of torture, when they first encounter them on starting school.

Writing picture books is therefore a worthwhile – and an enjoyable – occupation. Be warned, though, that it's not as easy as it looks. I've seen people flip through a picture book with only a few words on each page and mutter, "Good heavens, anyone could do this. It's money for old rope!" In fact the simplicity is deceptive. Like an iceberg with only the tip showing, there's a lot going on beneath the surface.

A world of wonder and delight

If you are a parent or a grandparent or even a godparent, you are no doubt well acquainted with the amazing quality and range of books available today for small children. They include board books, pop-up books, nursery rhymes, bedtime stories, alphabet books and activity books, as well as every story theme you can think of. There seems no end to the inventiveness of authors like Eric Carle, whose *Very Hungry Caterpillar* literally eats his way through the pages of the book; or Janet and Allan Ahlberg, whose

Jolly Postman delivers a postbag of real letters – or Christmas cards – which children can open up and read. Especially popular at the moment are those where the reader is invited to "lift the flap", such as Eric Hill's *Spot* books.

So how on earth do you find a fresh approach?

Well, for a start you can try to avoid climbing on somebody else's bandwaggon. One editor told me that the number of imitation *Postman Pat* books she'd been sent was unbelievable. Much the same goes for *Paddington* and *Thomas the Tank Engine*.

It's also important to bear in mind that full colour picture books are expensive to produce, and in order to make them viable publishers need to be sure of international sales. This means that your book must have a universal appeal, and for that reason it's advisable to avoid references to national institutions, such as double-decker buses or baseball, which may not mean very much to a child from Holland or the Gambia. If, however, you take a closer look at what's on offer you may come to some interesting conclusions.

What kind of a book?

There is a bewildering choice. When you study the market more closely you will soon realise that 0-7 is a pretty wide age range, and needs to be subdivided into smaller groups of 0-3, 3-5 and 5-7, although obviously there will be a certain amount of overlapping. The text can vary in length, but is usually between 200 and 1,000 words.

You will also realise that, however short the text, the same principles apply as for children's fiction in general. In other words, the story is what matters most – and I use the word "story" intentionally. Although some of the simplest books may seem to have a theme rather than a plot, there's still a progression of ideas towards a satisfying conclusion. They follow a pattern; and this is the age when patterns are not only desirable, but of paramount importance.

And yes, your central character still needs to have some kind of a problem that must be solved, or an obstacle to overcome, before the end of the book. Obviously this problem must be one that your young readers can identify with, for example fear of the dark, and it needs to be handled at an appropriate level. What's more, you have to achieve this within a far tighter framework, which means that all your narrative skills will be needed to bring it off.

Subject matter

Almost anything, whether animate or inanimate, can be the central character in a children's book. Val Biro's *Gumdrop*, for example, is a vintage car. Inevitably, stories about animals abound, with bears (teddy or otherwise), cats, dogs and rabbits coming top in the popularity stakes. However, my local children's librarian often bemoans the fact that, when she wants something to read aloud to groups of small children, all she can find are books about animals. "I wish I could find more books that look at the world from a child's viewpoint," she says.

Shirley Hughes is a writer who manages brilliantly to do just that. Her stories show small children against an easily recognisable background, coping with the sort of problems that small children have to cope with, such as going to live in a new neighbourhood in *Moving Mollie*, or the loss of a dearly loved toy in *Dogger*. Even something as simple as a burst water pipe can form the basis of an Alfie adventure in *An Evening at Alfie's*. She says: "Picture books are a very good way of having a dialogue with a child. I'm simply amazed by the way children can take a story and make it their own, using it as a way of reinforcing their own experience of life as well as a starting point for their own stories and pictures".

Illustrations

Looking at the work of Shirley Hughes brings us face to face with a major consideration when it comes to writing picture books, since she provides both text and pictures. In fact she started her professional life as an illustrator and only later discovered that writing the words as well gave her a satisfying degree of control over the finished product.

Clearly if you are both an imaginative writer *and* a gifted artist you start with an enormous advantage, but what if you can't draw for toffee? Should you do the best you can and send your efforts off with your story to give the publisher some idea of what you have in mind? Or should you team up with a friend who can draw a bit, or perhaps even find an illustrator whose work you like and write to them care of their publishers?

The answer to all these questions is no. Writing to a well-known illustrator is not a good idea: the chances are they already have a full workload for many months to come. And, if you send your own or your friend's amateur efforts, your story may be turned down because of the pictures. Far better to submit the text without pictures and let the publishers match you with an artist already known to them. Indeed, it's quite possible they may be looking out for a good story for an artist they want to use.

Picture plus words

Whether you're an author-and-artist combined or just an author, the main requirement is that you should be able to think in terms of pictures. This may sound obvious: in fact it demands a totally different technique from any other form of storytelling. Once I was asked to supply the idea for a series of stories told entirely in pictures. Great! I thought; no words at all – that'll be a piece of cake. To my surprise it turned out to be the hardest thing I've ever attempted.

Writing a picture book is not the same as writing a short story. If you look at some books for the very young and try to imagine the text – sometimes only a few words to a page – without the pictures, you will realise that it can't be done. The real quality of the book lies in the combination of words *and* pictures, which together form a cohesive whole. Even though it may be the visual image that makes the greatest impact, the illustration can only exist as part of the original concept, which came from the author of the book – and I use the word "author" in the sense of originator. The words may be simple – the concept anything but.

If you divorced the text from the pictures of one of my favourite books, *Princess Smartypants* by Babette Cole, you'd get a very odd idea of the story. For example, when the text states that Princess Smartypants asked one of her suitors, Prince Rushford, to feed her pets, it's not until you look at the picture that you realise her "pets" are all fearsome prehistoric monsters. And when the text tells us that she suggested to Prince Fetlock that "he might like to put her pony through its paces", the picture shows the pony kicking up its heels and the Prince sailing through the air. Clearly the lesson to be learned is that you, as author, cannot simply write down a story and hand it over for someone else to illustrate. You must first visualise it as a whole and get it clear in your mind so that you can convey to the illustrator how the words and pictures will work together.

Ideally, the world depicted in the illustrations will be rich in possibilities for exploration. In Pat Hutchins' *Rosie's Walk*, now a modern classic, Rosie the hen takes a seemingly innocent walk through the farmyard, but children listening to the story will be able to spot for themselves the fox who's waiting to pounce on her. And in *Not now, Bernard* by David McKee all Bernard's attempts to get his busy parents' attention fail dismally, even when he tells them he's about to be eaten by a monster. Here the words and pictures are working in tandem, but are not both doing the same job.

You will, of course, need plenty of action to add variety to the pictures. Pages where the characters are engaged in static conversation, however lively, will give the illustrator nothing to get his teeth into. There's a temptation, when you first begin, to tell the story in slowly moving stages like the frames of an animated cartoon. In fact each picture should be complete in itself and contain a "happening": you don't need to show us your characters walking from one scene to the next.

Layout of a picture book

The number of pages in a picture book is governed by the way the paper is folded and can therefore be 16, 24 or 32 pages long – in other words, rising in multiples of eight. As a rough guide, a baby board book is usually 16 pages long, whereas most picture books have 24 or 32 pages. Allowing for the fact that the first two pages will be taken up with titles, etc, this leaves you with 14, 22 or 30 to play with. If you want to have a few double-page spreads, remember that they must always start with an even-numbered page; eg pp 10 and 11. This may seem so obvious as to be hardly worth mentioning, but it is something I had to learn the hard way.

It is a good idea to work out a rough storyboard by writing the number of pages down one side of a piece of paper, leaving plenty of room to describe each picture. Or, if you prefer, you can write the story first and then subdivide it into pages. Be prepared to play about with the words for a long time before you get the balance right: your first attempt will almost certainly be either too long or too short. Diana Kimpton says that she probably spends at least ten times as long revising as she does on the initial writing.

What happens next depends entirely on how accomplished an artist you are. If you are intending to do your own illustrations then you should complete, say, three samples, accompanied by a fair copy of your text and a brief description of the concept as a whole. However, sending off your original artwork could be risky: better to have some colour photocopies done and send those. Whether or not you complete all the illustrations before sending it out depends how confident you are of acceptance. It could be a total waste of time if, for example, the editor thinks the rabbit should be pink rather than blue, so it's better to wait until the idea is sold and the details formalised. In any case a publisher will be able to tell from your samples whether or not your work is likely to be of interest to him.

If you are sending the text alone you should include any picture or layout details you consider essential. It's best to let the illustrator decide any non-essential details. There's no need to show the layout of words on each page unless there's something unusual about it which you need to demonstrate.

Rhythm and repetition

In books that are designed for reading aloud by an adult there are no real limitations as far as vocabulary is concerned since any difficult words can be explained by the reader. Nonetheless the choice of words – and their arrangement on the page – is of major importance. In the discipline it imposes on the writer it is rather like writing poetry: the fewer the words you use the more crucial it becomes to get them right.

Sadly, these days stories told in rhyme are not popular with publishers because they don't translate easily into another language. However, this doesn't mean that any poetic skills you possess need be wasted. It's as important as ever to be aware of the power of language and the effect it can have on your reader. Good rhythm makes the book fun to listen to and fun to read – an important point when parents are asked to read a book for the hundredth time.

It helps if you have a natural ear for the rhythms of speech. The language you use needn't necessarily be simple, but it should be direct. Avoid falling into the trap of using phrases such as "Up went the fox" and "Down goes she", which employ the kind of syntax no child is likely to encounter in everyday life. But don't be afraid to introduce the odd eccentric, even newly-invented word, especially if it's onomatopoeic, such as the "rumpeta, rumpeta, rumpeta" of the elephant running down the road in Elfrida Vipont's *The Elephant and the Bad Baby*.

Which leads us on to the magical three. Have you noticed how often the number three crops up in fairy stories? There are always three brothers, or three princesses, or three wishes. It's partly a way of building up tension, making us wait while the two older brothers fail in the task they are set so that we are desperate for the youngest to succeed. It also satisfies that deep-seated need we all have to know that life has a underlying structure and isn't really such a higgledy-piggledy affair as it often seems to be.

"Please will you read it again?" is the best accolade any book can receive. Some stories hold an endless fascination for small readers and they never tire of hearing them over and over again. This is because they find the familiar reassuring; and repetition within the story itself helps to reinforce that sense of security: most children love to join in with lists and repeated lines. For this reason it's vital to read your picture book texts aloud to yourself so that you can hear the rhythm and if necessary fine tune the structure until you get it exactly right.

Repetition also provides another way of building up the tension as the story nears its climax. In John Burningham's *Mr Gumpy's Outing* Mr Gumpy takes his boat out on the river and is joined by a procession of different creatures, including children, a sheep, a rabbit and a goat. To each one he affably gives instructions not to muck about too much, while all the time the boat is becoming more and more dangerously overloaded. The ending is inevitable – but not of course disastrous.

Satisfying endings

The ending of a picture book is very important. What you need is the "Ah!" factor, that pleasurable sigh a reader gives when a story has been rounded off in a way that is deeply satisfying. It's no use leaving any loose threads, as you can when writing for older children: everything must be neatly tied up and every character safely home, no matter how terrifying their adventures may have been. On the other hand it's important to stop when the point of satisfaction has been reached: there's no need to spin it out by describing everyone sitting down to tea together. The conclusion of Diana Kimpton's enchanting story, *The Bear Father Christmas Forgot*, which leaves the bear finally united with the small girl whose Christmas present he was destined to be, is both triumphant and moving – not a dry eye in the house.

All very well, you may say, but what about a book like *Not now, Bernard* where the story ends with Bernard actually being devoured by the monster? Nothing particularly cosy or reassuring about that! And yet most children love it, because it's funny. The ha-ha! factor makes it acceptable.

The problem lies partly in the width of the age range covered by picture books. Obviously, what is acceptable to a seven-year-old may be deeply upsetting for a three-year-old, which is why you need to be aware who you are writing for. However, it's not only a matter of age but also of temperament: what is disturbing for one child may be a source for glee for another, and this is something the writer cannot possibly foresee. All you can do is make it clear what kind of a story it is right from the beginning, so that the adult buying the book is not taken by surprise. To tack a horrific ending on to what has been a fairly gentle story would be a betrayal of trust. Likewise, too tame an ending to a fantastical tale would disappoint the reader. Knowing when to take risks is largely a matter of experience, and perhaps on the whole it's best not to try pushing out the boundaries with your first attempt, but stick to the traditional happy ending.

To sum up:

1. Learn to think in terms of pictures.
2. Let your text complement the illustrations, not describe them.
3. Build up the tension with rhythm and repetition.
4. Read your text aloud and fine tune where it doesn't work.
5. Make sure your ending has the "Ah!" factor.

YOUNG FICTION (6-9)

If you find the prospect of writing a full length children's novel daunting, why not try your hand at something shorter and more manageable? First Readers, also known as Read Alone books, have become enormously popular in the last few years, ever since publishers woke up to the fact that there was a gap in the market. Making the transition from picture books to full length fiction is an important step for children who have just learned to read. Clearly what they need are good quality storybooks of an intermediate length, exciting enough to hold their interest and challenging enough to test and extend their newly acquired skill.

Great news for young readers, then, but what are the chances for writers?

I would be misleading you if I suggested it was easy to break into this field. The competition is very hot indeed, with writers of the calibre of Anne Fine, Penelope Lively, Dick King-Smith – to name but a few – all contributing work up to their usual high standard. However, the demand is so great that, whereas at one time most stories were specially commissioned from writers with a proven track record, editors are now more than willing to consider unsolicited manuscripts. Be warned, though – these must be of an outstanding quality to have a hope of being accepted.

So, how do you achieve this outstanding quality?

Market research

Sorry to trot out such a hoary old piece of advice, but this is an area where doing your research is even more vital than usual.

Before you begin you must know what the publishers' requirements are, because they can vary considerably. Some do not want too much dialogue; others like plenty and it must be as lively as possible. Some ask specifically for plenty of humour. You can learn a lot from browsing in bookshops and libraries: note especially the intriguing titles, such as *Emily's Legs* (Macdonald Storybooks) and *The Phantom Carwash* (Banana), which combined with bright, jazzy covers are just the thing to catch a young reader's eye. It is also helpful to get hold of some catalogues: publishers are usually happy to send you one on request and may even supply a tip sheet.

From your research you will soon discover that the books vary in length from 1,000 to 7,500 words and are generally aimed at the 6-9 age group. For example, Hamish Hamilton publish three series: Cartwheels (1,000 words) designed to be the next step up from a picture book; Gazelles (4000 words), intended to boost children's confidence in reading a whole book; and Antelopes (7,500 words), a more substantial read for the top end of the age group. First Readers can also be subdivided according to genre rather than age group: Scholastic have several series such as Young Hippo Magic, Young Hippo Spooky and Young Hippo Adventure.

You will also realise there is a considerable variation in house style. For example, A & C Black's *Jets* are particularly lively, using all sorts of narrative devices such as speech balloons and cartoon strips. The interest level also varies: some series are quite sophisticated in content whereas others tend to use a simpler approach. All are lavishly illustrated, some in full colour but most with black and white line illustrations breaking up the words on each page.

But what if you have written a story for this age group that won't fit into any existing slot? Well, there is still a market for individual novels, but on the whole publishers do tend to think in terms of series. An alternative is to initiate your own series about a particularly memorable character or group of characters, such as Jill Murphy's *Worst Witch* stories. You can even do this under the umbrella of an established series, such as Sheila Lavelle's *Ursula Bear* stories which are published as *Gazelles*.

By now you will appreciate how important it is to do your research. This is a highly specialised field and if you want to break into it you need to know exactly where your book is likely to fit into the existing market.

The importance of being sparky

The next thing you need is a really scintillating idea. The subject can be anything – space, pirates, contemporary family and school life, magic, animals, ghosts and mystery, monsters, whatever takes your fancy. The main requirement is that it must give you plenty of scope for writing visually: these books require plenty of action, something happening on every page. Take a look at Valerie Wilding's hilarious stories about Prince Vince, royal detective (Hodder Story Books). From the opening paragraph of *Prince Vince and the Case of the Smelly Goat*, when the butler Macclesfield says an unbelievably rude word in front of the Royal Family, there is never a dull moment as Prince Vince follows his nose to find the kidnapped Mucky Bucky, the smelliest goat in the land.

When choosing your subject it is important to keep in mind that you are writing for today's children, whose tastes tend not only to be catholic but also fairly sophisticated. This doesn't necessarily mean that fairy stories are out, but it is advisable to give them a modern twist. Even if you take a well-worn theme you can always try turning it upside down or inside out – anything to breathe new life into it. Publishers especially like stories which reflect our multicultural society. In Marjorie Newman's *Green Monster Magic* (Rooster) for example, Estelle's small brother Joseph is scared stiff at the thought of acting in the school play, especially as his grandmother is coming all the way from Africa to see him. And it is Grandmother's re-telling of a Nigerian story that gives Estelle the key to helping Joseph overcome his fear.

One word of warning: when writing for this age group we are usually at pains to create a fictional world that is safe, friendly and comforting. Unfortunately the real world is very different and on the whole it is safer to avoid putting our fictional characters into a potentially dangerous situation, such as accepting a lift from a stranger. In *Stranger Danger* (Gazelle) Anne Fine tackles the problem head-on with humour and sensitivity, but it would be quite wrong to use such a situation as a mere narrative ploy to further the plot.

Whatever the subject matter, you need to find an original approach, the freshness of appeal that will give your story its outstanding quality. Above all, the purpose of these books is to entertain: a predictable story-line and a leaden prose style could easily put a child off reading for life. So try to bear in mind the importance of being sparky.

A novel in miniature

From your research you will have discovered that most of the longer stories are divided into chapters. For example, a 2,500-word story will probably have four chapters; a 7,500-word story may have six. This helps to give the feel of a real book, as well as breaking it up into manageable sections. It also helps to remind you, the writer, that what you are attempting to produce is not a short story, but a novel in miniature.

This means that it's important to achieve some depth of characterisation. If your central character is a child, take care that he or she comes across as a well rounded, believable person, and not as a two dimensional goody-goody who could not possibly exist in real life. Adults, too, need to be strongly drawn. The more vividly you can bring them to life the more memorable they will be – and the more your illustrator will enjoy drawing them.

You also need quite a meaty plot, rich with dramatic possibilities. To give you an example, in my own story *Alberta* (Antelope) my eponymous heroine, a small white furry abominable snowthing from the arctic wastes of Canada, is captured while hibernating and shipped to a zoo in England. However there is a mix-up with two crates, and she is delivered instead to a boy called Felix, who is expecting a quite different present from his father. Alberta's shock on waking up to find herself far from home and family provided me with the emotional springboard for the plot; while Felix's attempts to keep the presence of this odd-looking creature a secret gave me plenty of scope for comedy.

The art of simplicity

Your narrative should be imaginative but simple, with a single, continuous thread to carry the reader through from beginning to end without sub plots, lengthy description or introspection. The beginning, of course, is vital: you must grab your readers right away and pull them quickly into the story. What you need is a dramatic situation that sets both the scene and the tone of the whole book, so that the reader can tell from the first page that this is going to be a story worth persevering with.

It helps if the text is broken up into plenty of paragraphs, rather than presented as a solid block. There are no limitations as to vocabulary, but it is important to bear in mind that too many long words or involved sentences are discouraging for a struggling new reader. In fact it is an excellent test of your ability to write clearly and directly, without the slightest need to lower your literary standards. Take a look at how some of the experts tackle the task and you will see what I mean.

Dividing the story into chapters is helpful not only for the reader but also for the writer. It provides a framework on which you can build, by means of a series of dramatic scenes and incidents, towards a satisfying conclusion. You know that in that first chapter, as when writing a longer novel, you have to establish your main characters. You also know that each chapter should end on a high point, a question mark that will make your reader keep turning the pages. I always find that, although I may have a vague idea of how the story will develop, it isn't until I start arranging it in chapters that I can see the overall shape. Then I know exactly how I should proceed.

When you have finished your story try reading it aloud, either to yourself or to a sympathetic listener to see if it works. If it is too long go through it again, pruning out all the unnecessary adjectives and adverbs and even whole sentences if they are superfluous. Only when you have reduced it to a tight, well constructed piece without an ounce of spare flesh on its bones, will you be ready to send it off to your chosen publisher.

To sum up:

1. Research thoroughly all the current series.
2. Think up a really scintillating idea.
3. Make sure this idea is meaty enough to make a complete miniature novel.
4. Keep your narrative simple but lively.
5. Check you've wasted no words – and no opportunity to be entertaining.

10

GENERAL FICTION (8-11)

When it comes to the area of general fiction the boundaries are less clearly defined. Here there is far more scope for the one-off novel; or at least there is at present. As in the field of adult fiction, publishers are tending more and more to think in terms of genres, finding that a book marketed under the heading of "horror", or "mystery" or "ghost story" is more likely to appeal to a young reader who may not have heard of the author. These are the cold hard facts of publishing. Nonetheless this is still an area where quality counts and if a truly original, well-written book lands on an editor's desk they will be more than ready to take a risk on it.

The most usual length for general fiction is 10,000 – 25,000 words, although it can be as much as 60,000 words if the book is of outstanding literary quality. However these days, for economic reasons, it is very rare to find a children's novel of more than 40,000 words, so you would be well advised to keep your first attempt within these limits. Chapters should also be on the short side, depending on the type of book you are writing. For example, a story of about 25,000 words would probably be divided into about fifteen chapters.

Whatever kind of book you are writing, all the narrative skills described in the earlier part of this book will be needed, ie good characterisation, pace, style, drama and natural-sounding dialogue. If you stop thinking of it in terms of "a children's book" and start applying the same criteria as you would if you were writing an adult novel you won't go far wrong. Sometimes I think we tend to underestimate children's ability to grasp quite complex ideas. Left to their own devices, they often choose to read the most unexpected books by authors who certainly never set out to be "children's writers".

Avoid the ordinary

When it comes to this age group, way ahead in the popularity stakes is the inimitable Roald Dahl. No matter what his adult critics may say, children know that he is *on their side*. They feel drawn into a kind of conspiracy, perhaps because there is a subversive element in his books. A direct descendant of the brothers Grimm, he glories in the macabre and revels in the outrageous.

The lesson to be learned from Dahl, and from so many other popular authors, is that if you want to make your mark it's no use playing safe. You have to be prepared to go out on a limb. What your story needs in order to make publishers and readers alike sit up and take notice is that special quality – call it freshness, or energy or what you will – that lifts it head and shoulders above the dozens of other unsolicited manuscripts an editor receives each week. It's no use trotting out a tired old plot that has been used hundreds of times before.

To give you an example, let's imagine you want to write a story about two children running away. The first questions you will ask yourself are what – or who – are they running away *from* and where are they running *to*? Well, there are all sorts of answers, most of them fairly predictable – unless, that is, you're a writer of the calibre of E.L. Konigsburg. In her book, *From the Mixed up Files of Mrs Basil E. Frankweiler* the two children run away because they are bored and take up residence in New York's Metropolitan Museum of Art, hiding from the officials and acquiring an intimate knowledge of Michelangelo. Nothing predictable there.

Cynthia Voigt, on the other hand, turns it into an epic quest story in *Homecoming* when four children, abandoned by their mentally ill mother, journey from Connecticut to Maryland to find the grandmother they have never met. And in Gillian Cross's *The Great Elephant Chase*, the two children race across America with Khush the elephant, pursued by the dastardly Hannibal Jackson.

In other words, try to avoid the ordinary. By that I don't mean that every book has to have an exotic setting and unexpected twists in the plot, merely that you should find a fresh approach, a new way of looking at an old idea, that will give your book the "something extra" it needs to succeed in this competitive market.

Family situations

Many books for this middle age group are concerned with family situations, or are at least set against the background of a family. As we are all aware, marriage break-ups, single parents and step families are now the norm rather than the exception, and this – quite rightly – is reflected in children's fiction. Indeed, I once heard a mother complain that she couldn't find any books for her daughter to read featuring children with a stable family background like their own.

There are many variations in family structure that can be rewarding to explore. In my Miranda books, Miranda's mother is trying to scrape a living as a cab-driver while her husband is in prison for fraud, a situation which makes the relationship between mother and daughter particularly significant. And when I came to write a ghost story, *The Haunting of Gull Cottage*, I decided to ring the changes on the old five-children-and-a-dog routine by making three of them foster-children, which again created an intriguing tension within the family. (I kept the dog, but he played an important part in the story and wasn't just there for decoration.)

To my mind, every book needs a touch of mystery – and this applies as much to stories with a family background as it does to whodunnits. Family secrets are a great source of drama, and no character with any depth comes without baggage from the past. The need to find out what makes people tick, and to explore all kinds of relationships, is one of the main reasons why children read. Life itself is a mysterious business and trying to make sense of it is what we are programmed to do.

Today's children tend to be remarkably clear-eyed about what goes on in their own homes and to offer them fiction which is less than honest would be selling them short. However, I do feel quite strongly that, when writing for this age group, we should be careful not to burden them with too much *angst*. Inevitably much of what we write will touch on certain social and moral "issues", but again, it's not so much what you say as the way you say it. At all costs, try to avoid climbing on your soap-box. Any tendency to preachiness should be firmly suppressed.

A spirit of adventure

In the good old days, when writing an adventure story, it was common practice to keep the parents well in the background, or even get rid of them altogether, so that the children could get on with the plot unimpeded. Sadly, these days it is no longer realistic to let children roam the countryside alone or visit strange old women who live deep in the wood.

So how careful do we have to be?

Publishers vary considerably in their views on this issue. Some are not too bothered about it; others prefer to tread with caution. Clearly, as writers, we have a responsibility here. Nonetheless it can be very limiting if your child characters are never allowed out of the house on their own, let alone to make any kind of an epic journey. There are, however, certain ways of getting round the problem.

For a start, it's best to send your characters out in pairs, or even in groups, especially if they are investigating some kind of a mystery that involves adults. Don't let them tangle with dangerous criminals, especially those carrying arms; and if it's a smuggling tale, avoid drugs. These are all very hackneyed plot devices anyway. Perhaps the reason why ghost stories are comparatively free of this problem is that the danger invariably comes from within.

You can also distance the action in various ways. For example, Gillian Cross set *The Great Elephant Chase* back in time, at the end of the nineteenth century. Or your central character may not be a child: it can be an adult, as in a science fiction adventure, or even an animal. When it comes to fantasy, of course, your hero or heroine is free to go anywhere and do anything, which is probably why it is becoming such a popular form with writers weary of restrictions. Even a fairly realistic fantasy, where the characters may be larger than life but the situations are basically recognisable, will give you plenty of scope.

In the end it is a matter for your own judgement. If you want to deal with a controversial situation and feel that the constraints are unreasonable, then you must write as you wish and try to find a publisher who shares your views.

Modern living

When writing for this age group it is important to bear in mind that the pace of life has changed, for children just as much as for adults. Although many of the classics are as popular as ever, it is often necessary when reading them aloud to condense the longer descriptive passages, otherwise the audience may become restive. For better or for worse, we live in a television age. Children are used to receiving stories in a series of short, dramatic scenes, and the modern children's book reflects this trend.

Literary styles have changed too. Today's writers are not too bothered about correct grammar: at least, not to the point of pedantry. Their narrative technique is more relaxed and their dialogue crisp and realistic. People often deplore the fact that today's children have a limited vocabulary compared with their Victorian counterparts. This may be true, although it would perhaps be more accurate to say they have a *different* vocabulary: the Victorians never had to cope with computerese. Certainly as writers we should make our choice of language as rich and varied as possible, but not at the risk of confusing our readers.

When it comes to subject matter, how trendy should we try to be?

Obviously we need to be aware of children's current interests. However I feel it would be a bad mistake to base an entire book on something you don't thoroughly understand. Children are extremely knowledgeable on certain subjects and can soon spot a phoney who is trying to fudge it. When Malorie Blackman wrote *Hacker* about a computer fraud she knew exactly what she was doing – and it shows.

In the end, of course, our choice of subject matter will reflect our own preoccupations; and the way in which we tackle it will vary according to our personal style and temperament. We have to be true to ourselves as well as the age we are living in.

Working within a genre

Some find this restrictive, but in fact it offers a discipline which can be very helpful, especially for the novice writer. There are several crime writers who could undoubtedly make their name in a more literary field but choose to work within a specific genre. This doesn't necessarily mean that it's easier. On the contrary, you are aiming to please a highly critical readership who know what they like and won't be fobbed off with second best.

Nor does it mean you have to sacrifice your personal input, or your own particular style of writing. When asked to write a ghost story, I made myself think, *What is the greatest irrational fear that I have*? Now, if there's one thing I cannot bear it's being the same room as a fluttering bird. Bad enough if it's only a budgerigar, but supposing it was something really huge, like a raven? From that was born *The Nightmare Man*, subsequently published in the Hippo "Hauntings" series. What you need to guard against is the temptation to churn out a stereotypical plot because you think this is what is meant by a "genre novel". There is just as much need for originality in this as in any other field of writing.

All kinds of stereotyping, sexist or otherwise, should of course be strenuously avoided. It is undoubtedly a form of laziness, implying that you prefer to follow a hackneyed formula rather than take a fresh look at the world about you. On the other hand, there's no need to go over the top. Not all Mums need be nuclear physicists, nor all Dads wear aprons and do the housework. As long as you bear in mind that times have changed and stereotypes are boring, you should get the balance about right.

It is a good idea to aim for a particular series so that you can work within the publisher's guidelines as to length etc. This can save you a great deal of time and wasted effort: the closer you come to meeting their requirements the more likely they are to accept your book.

Nothing but the best

If you spend an hour or so browsing in the children's section of your local library you will soon become aware of the enormous variety of fiction available, far greater than in the adult section. This can be rather daunting, especially when you realise the quality of the competition, but it can also be a challenge. There is so much scope for you as a writer – far more, possibly, than you ever dreamed of.

It can also be a sobering exercise, however, to check how many times a book has been borrowed during the past year. Very often you find that many critically-acclaimed children's novels have hardly been taken out at all, whereas books by less highly rated writers boast columns and columns of date stamps. Of course it's easy to dismiss this by saying that these frequently-borrowed writers are clearly pandering to the popular taste. All the same, I can't see the point of being critically-acclaimed but unread. Surely, there has to be a happy medium?

Yes, there is; and many writers have managed to strike it. Diana Wynne Jones, Joan Aiken and Margaret Mahy all manage to hit exactly the right note with their young readers, while at the same time satisfying even the most critical adult. So here's another challenge – not only to write good books, but good books that children actually *want to read*.

To sum up:

1. Avoid the ordinary.
2. Set your standards high: nothing but the best will do.
3. Be honest: don't sell your readers short.
4. Relax and let your narrative style be natural.
5. Don't forget to add a touch of mystery.

11

MIND YOUR LANGUAGE!

When writing for children a lively prose style is essential. You owe it to your readers to be original, even adventurous, in your choice of words. Children are fascinated by language. They are still themselves at the experimental stage, trying out new words every day, which is why you shouldn't be afraid to use the occasional difficult word, provided its meaning is sufficiently clear from the context. I don't know how old I was when I first read Beatrix Potter's *Tale of the Flopsy Bunnies*, but it was the word "soporific" that made the strongest impression on me and I was never in any doubt as to what it meant. Similarly the Parsee's "Superior comestible" in Kipling's *Just So Stories*.

Clearly, though, it's not just a matter of vocabulary, although your choice of words is vitally important. In fact the fewer words you use the more carefully you have to choose them. But sentence structure is important too; and so is getting the rhythm right, especially if your stories are designed to be read aloud.

Structure and rhythm

Wherever possible try to avoid long, complex sentences full of conjunctions and subordinate clauses. The more direct you can make your writing style, the more impact it will have on the reader.

For this reason it is always best to put statements in a positive rather than a negative form, even if they are negative in content. For example, "*He ignored me*" would be preferable to "*He did not pay any attention to me*".

Wherever possible try to use the active voice rather than the passive. *"There was a large dog howling outside the door"* doesn't sound nearly so menacing as *"A large dog howled outside the door"*. And *"He raised the alarm"* is more dramatic than *"the alarm was raised"*.

Be specific. *"They ate a delicious meal"* doesn't tell your readers what they want to know. Food is important to children. Did this meal consist of fish and chips and jelly and ice-cream? Or burgers and chocolate cake? Lack of detail is the sign of a lazy writer. It's much easier to write *"The garden was full of flowers"* than to find out exactly which flowers might be in bloom at a particular time of year; whereas if you describe a *"riot of pink azalea"* or a *"drift of snowdrops beneath the cedar tree"* the image transmitted to your readers will be far more vivid, even if they're not quite sure what an azalea looks like.

As for rhythm, a writer's sense of euphony is largely a matter of instinct. If you are uncertain, try reading your work aloud, preferably to somebody else. Does the stress fall in the right places? Are there any examples of clumsy construction that make you stumble when reading? Any jarring notes or awkward combination of words? You may need to write and rewrite a sentence several times before you are entirely happy with it. This is where the *craft* of writing comes in: the natural, unforced style that is the hallmark of a good writer is actually an illusion, achieved only after hours of tinkering with the text until it satisfies his innate sense of harmony.

Tailoring your style

One of the trickiest aspects for novice writers is knowing how to tailor your work to suit the age and ability of your readers. To some extent this is again a matter of instinct: the letter you write to your eleven-year-old nephew will differ both in content and in style from the letter you write to his four-year-old sister. You'll have changed gear without even having to think about it. But what if you're writing for a host of nephews and nieces you've never met? How can you be sure you're hitting the right note?

Perhaps the first question you should ask yourself is, *Am I absolutely clear in my own mind which age group I'm writing for?*

This may sound elementary, but you'd be surprised how many people describe their stories simply as being "for children", as if all children, from 0-11, can be lumped together. It's true that dividing them into age groups is a somewhat arbitrary exercise, since their needs and abilities will inevitably overlap: a ten-year-old with reading difficulties may settle down happily with a book aimed at seven-year-olds. Nonetheless it's advisable, before firing your arrow into the air, to make sure it's pointing in roughly the right direction.

It may be helpful to look at a single incident – the discovery of hoof prints on a sandy beach – as it might be tailored to suit the three main age groups.

1. A picture book
   (Illustration shows Sarah, aged about 4, walking barefoot on a beach.)
   Sarah loved walking over the warm sand. Wherever she trod she left a neat footprint, showing her round heel and five toes. But look! There was another footprint in the sand – a large, round one without any toes. Who could have made it?

Here the illustrations will be doing most of the story-telling, but that doesn't mean the words don't matter. However, there's no point in having your words describe exactly what is happening in the picture. *"Sarah was walking across the beach"* would only be stating what the readers can see for themselves. The task of the writer is to bring out the sensations and emotions of the situation. *"Sarah loved walking over the warm sand"* complements the illustration by telling us how and what she's feeling.

2. A first reader
   (Illustration shows Sarah, now aged 8.)
   Sarah stared down at the sand. She saw first one hoofprint ... and another and another ... then a whole line of hoofprints stretching far across the bay. The strange thing was that they seemed to start at the water's edge. Could a horse have come galloping out of the sea?

As in the first version, the situation needs to be made as dramatic as possible. Nor should you hesitate to use any kind of linguistic device that will emphasise the drama. For example repetition, as in *"She saw first one hoofprint ... and another and another."*

The real hazard at this stage is sentence structure. Admittedly you don't want to use too many short, staccato sentences, but neither should you make them too long and convoluted. A new young reader can easily become lost amidst a jungle of complicated clauses. Anything that starts off: *"Running along the road, and very frightened, Peter ..."* is bound to confuse. It also lacks immediacy.

3. A full length novel
   (No illustration.)
   The beach was empty, new-washed by the tide. I am the first living creature ever to set foot upon this sand, Sarah thought as she ran down to the water's edge. But then she noticed a line of hoofprints coming out of the sea and realised she was not the first. A horse had been here before her, with or without a rider. She followed the hoofprints along the deserted shore until eventually they disappeared again, into the sea. How strange ...

By now you should be using your sentence structure to control the pace and atmosphere of your writing. Again, it's safer to err on the side of simplicity. Many writers use the dreaded participial clause primarily to avoid using the word "and". Instead of: *"But then she noticed a line of hoofprints coming out of the sea and realised she was not the first"* I could have put: *"Noticing a line of hoofprints coming out of the sea, she realised she was not the first."* My literary instincts, though, tell me that the present participle should be used sparingly.

I don't mind admitting that, in the first version of the story, I agonised for some while over *"she left a neat footprint, showing her round heel ..."* But the alternative would have been *"...she left a neat footprint which showed ..."* Even worse!

The stories will develop, as you can see, along very different lines. The picture book version deals with a small, child-centred world; the first reader and the full length novel gradually extend that vision, like widening ripples on a lake. All three versions are dramatic, but there are important differences between them.

"Bad" language

Have you stood in or near a school playground recently? If you have, you will be well aware of the kind of aggressive language children use in everyday life. To a great many of them swearing is a natural form of communication, which means that when we come to write naturalistic dialogue in a contemporary story we're faced with something of a dilemma.

How true-to-real-life should we try to be?

A lot depends on your publisher. Some are quite happy to print a few "bloody"s and "sod"s, whereas others will edit them out. Anything more extreme might land you in difficulty, but you could always try to negotiate on the grounds that it's essential to your story and not meretricious. Be warned, though: over-use of expletives can result in letters of complaint to teachers, librarians and even publishers.

You have to bear in mind that although swearing is a part of many children's lives at school, different standards may operate at home. To my mind it's safer to steer a middle course rather than risk giving unnecessary offence. However, the goal posts are constantly being moved and what gives offence today may be perfectly acceptable tomorrow.

Some common grammatical problems

Grammar is a tricky area, mainly because fashions change and we are no longer always certain what is correct and what isn't. For example, in a modern story it would sound pedantic to say "with whom" or "for whom"; and it is no longer incorrect to begin a sentence with "and" or "but", or to have a sentence without a verb. Nonetheless we all stumble from time to time, usually over the same knotty little problems. Here are a few of them:

1. Use of the subjunctive. Should you say "He wished he were free" or "He wished he *was* free"? In the past the subjunctive was used when expressing a wish rather than a fact, but these days it's regarded as unnecessary. So it's up to you to choose whichever you think sounds best.

2. Possessive apostrophe. Should it be "Charles' book" or "Charles's book"? These days it is accepted practice to add 's whatever the final consonant, so you should use "Charles's book", "St James's Place", "Dickens's novels", etc.

3. Use of the pluperfect. If we are describing something that happened in the past must we use the cumbersome "had" throughout? For example, "Last December Julia had visited her aunt and had found her ill and undernourished. She had cooked her a meal and thoroughly cleaned the flat, but when she had tried to persuaded her aunt to have Meals on Wheels she had failed." The answer is no, the first "had" is enough to establish that it happened in the past: for the rest of the paragraph you can drop the pluperfect and use the plain past tense.

4. The dreaded participial clause again. "Having crossed the Atlantic, a crowd waited for him at the jetty". This suggests it was the crowd that had crossed the Atlantic, which is possible but unlikely. The opening phrase must relate to the subject of the sentence. It should read: "Having crossed the Atlantic, he found a crowd waiting for him at the jetty."

I must admit that I still wince at split infinitives. The most famous example comes from Star Trek – "to boldly go" – but if you trying changing it to the more grammatically correct "to go boldly" or "boldly to go" it doesn't have the same dramatic impact. I also wince at the use of "different to" instead of "different from"; "quite unique"; and the confusion of "infer" and "imply". But then we all have our grammatical hangups and I daresay you could add to this list. The inescapable fact is that grammar is changing all the time, and for this reason it would be foolish to be too fussy about its correct or incorrect use. On the other hand, writing for children does put us in something of a quandary.

For example, the mistakes children most commonly make in their everyday speech are: "me and John", "might *of* been", and "fed up *of*". Now, when aiming to write realistic dialogue, should we reproduce these mistakes at the risk of perpetuating them; or should we make our child characters speak impeccable English?

Well, it's your choice. For my part, I have used "me and John", making it clear that it's a kind of joke, but not the others. Mind you, I might at some time in the future make use of them, if the situation demanded it. In the end, it's a matter of personal judgement.

If you would like some professional guidance through the language labyrinth, I suggest you get hold of *The Elements of Style* by Strunk & White. And yes, that is the same E.B.White who wrote *Charlotte's Web*, which is the best possible recommendation you could have.

12

YOUNG ADULTS

The young adult market has been through a difficult patch, and although some excellent books have been published in the last few years, sales generally fell off so much that publishers became wary of buying new manuscripts. Recently, however, it has undergone something of a revival, largely due to the advent of Scholastic's Point Horror series, which is currently enjoying a phenomenal popularity with children from about 9 to 15. Teachers and librarians tend to be less enthusiastic: booksellers, needless to say, are delighted.

For writers too it has to be good news that the market has come back to life. The hope is that this born-again interest in reading will have a knock-on effect, encouraging young people to widen their interests and rediscover the wealth of good fiction available to them. What they need is a book that will not only hold their interest but also widen their horizons and deepen their understanding of human relationships – and this is exactly what the best of young adult fiction sets out to do.

Who are these "young adults"?

Once upon a time they were known as teenagers. More recently they have been termed "new adults" or, more commonly, "young adults" and are usually defined as being between 12 and 16 years of age. This, of course, is intended only as a rough guide: everyone accepts that children mature at different rates and cannot possibly be so neatly classified. It is also generally agreed that they vary enormously as regards intellectual ability and background, and it is therefore only right and proper that the books provided for them should reflect this difference and cater for their needs.

If there is a common denominator it must surely be the profound physical and emotional upheaval that marks the transition from childhood to adulthood. Like the younger children's need to test their courage by reading ghost and horror stories, adolescents also use books as a kind of sounding board. Reading how fictional characters cope with problems they may share, such as the agony of shyness or the difficulty of making parents realise they are no longer children, will at the very least make them feel they are not alone. At best, it may even help them find their way through the labyrinth.

If you were yourself a bookish child, you can probably remember that books were not only a great comfort to you at this time, but they also assumed an almost mystical significance. Salinger's *Catcher in the Rye*, for example, and William Golding's *Lord of the Flies*, both categorised as adult novels, are enormously popular with adolescents. Surely it is not mere coincidence that these two books are about self-discovery, and the seemingly impossible task of coming to terms with the adult world.

The best guide when choosing the theme of your book must surely to draw on your own experience as a teenager. Think back to your main preoccupations at that time and see how they can be translated into today's terms. Don't forget you'll have the advantage of being able to synthesize, making sense of what may at the time have seemed utter confusion. You can also use any expert knowledge you may have acquired along the way to enrich the background of the story, so that the situation you are dealing with can be fleshed out with interesting detail.

This means, inevitably, that you'll be looking at the situation from a subtly altered vantage point. Nonetheless, if you're writing about something that once made a deep impression on you, and are able to recreate the emotions you felt at the time, the chances are that your book will strike a chord in the mind of some receptive reader. Research has shown that what teenagers want is a good meaty read, something that will make them laugh or cry – and if both, so much the better.

No concessions

At the top end of the market you will find books that make little or no concession to mass popularity. These are aimed at the highly literate child and are intended to stretch and challenge the intellect. For this reason they may appeal equally to the discriminating adult, which is why most enlightened libraries stock such books both in the children's section and on the adult fiction shelves. Some, like Robert Cormier's *I am the Cheese*, use the kind of complex narrative technique more usually found in an adult novel. Others, like Alan Garner's *The Owl Service*, demand a high level of emotional understanding.

Complexity of ideas, of course, doesn't necessarily demand complexity of language. The best writers in this field have mastered the art of expressing themselves in clear, direct prose refreshingly free of literary mannerisms. The wonderfully liberating message for the writer is, therefore: Don't be afraid to set sail on difficult waters. Provided your vessel is seaworthy and you are prepared to trim your sails where necessary, there is really nothing to stop you going wherever you want to go.

A huge favourite with this age group – and here again the line between junior and adult fiction is blurred – is the fantasy writer Terry Pratchett. His jokey excursions into wizardry appeal to readers of all ages, which is surely the key to success when it comes to writing for young adults. If we stop thinking of our potential readers as children, and instead try to satisfy our own highest standards as to what makes a good read, we are far less likely to insult their intelligence. Recently I read a comment by a fifteen-year-old dismissing most teenage fiction as "patronising" and quite frankly I think he has a point.

The need for honesty

Another popular writer with this age group is Paula Danziger. This may be partly due to her style – light and entertaining, with never a hint of pomposity – and partly to the honest way she deals with the trials and tribulations experienced by adolescents. Cassie, in *The Pistachio Prescription*, has impossible parents, a gorgeous-looking older sister and a brother who is everybody's favourite. She also has asthma. For all these problems her favourite remedy is to eat pistachio nuts, which she keeps hidden away for break-down situations.

Kitty, in Anne Fine's award-winning *Goggle-eyes*, also has problems. The *Goggle-eyes* of the title is Gerald, her divorced mother's new boyfriend, who seems far too staid and conventional to fit into their chaotic, campaigning life-style. What on earth can her mother be thinking about? Here again, the situation is treated with humour, compassion and an honesty that lifts it far above the average run of books about teenage *angst*.

Publishers are constantly looking out for books that deal realistically with the world we live in. They would love to receive more manuscripts from writers who have first-hand experience of growing up in a multi-racial society, especially those from ethnic minorities. But bear in mind the advice given by Beverley Anderson in the Good Book Guide to Children's Books:

> What matters is that "multicultural" books should be as interesting and well-written as any others and that they can be enjoyed by the children who come from the communities they describe without embarrassment, anxiety or irritation. A feebly plotted, clumsily written book by someone from the appropriate background is no more acceptable than a similar book by an outsider.

Two books she particularly recommends are Anita Desai's *The Village by the Sea* and Farrukh Dhondy's *Come to Mecca*.

Any theme, from politics to sexual and social problems, is acceptable, provided it is dealt with honestly and with sensitivity. It must be said, however, that books which set out to deal with specific sexual or social issues are not on the whole remarkable for their literary merit. Unfortunately, many of them have the unmistakable stamp of a "manufactured" book.

It would be unwise, therefore, to take a cool, calculated look at the market, decide the publishers are going for inner-city novels at the moment, and set about writing one without ever having lived in an inner city yourself. The result will almost certainly be unconvincing, peopled by the kind of "stock" characters you imagine may live in tower blocks but who are little more than caricatures. You can only write truthfully about what you know; and if your own experience seems to you not only limited but irrelevant, remember that not all children live in inner cities; and even those that do may enjoy reading about somewhere different for a change. It is far more important to get the emotional content of the book right, and you can only do that by writing from the heart. So put honesty first: it's by far the best policy.

Horror and Romance

On the face of it, these may appear to be odd bedfellows. The reason I have put them together is partly because they are the two most popular genres at the moment, and partly because in some ways they seem curiously to overlap.

At this age there has always been a divergence in the literary tastes of boys and girls, sometimes blamed on sexist stereotyping. A far more likely reason is that their physical and emotional responses to the onset of puberty are quite different. Whereas most boys like to imagine how they would cope with the kind of challenge to be found in the realms of horror, space fiction and thrillers, girls are more concerned with their ability to handle relationships.

While this is still largely true, any librarian will tell you that girls are almost as keen as boys on the new wave of horror stories. To some extent this may reflect the universal appetite for violence all too evident on our cinema and TV screens, but if you take a look at some of the fictional horror on offer you will find that some of it is really romance-in-disguise. A typical plot might feature a girl attracted to a handsome-but-strange new boy at school only to find that at midnight he turns into a vampire – but of course all he needs is the love of a good woman to break the spell.

When it comes to romance "proper", not all books can be lumped together. There is a vast difference between them, a fact that is sometimes obscured by unimaginative packaging. The jackets, presumably designed to catch the eye of a browsing teenager, are not always an accurate guide to what lies between the covers.

If you take a closer look you will find that while some are blatantly escapist, others attempt to offer good characterisation and a more honest approach to human relationships.

There are usually tipsheets available for novels in both genres, giving you some kind of guidance as to what is acceptable and what is not. In many romances aimed at the mass market, for example, the tone may be tender, funny, down-to-earth, but not sentimental, moralistic or graphically sexual. The style, while colloquial, should not include profanity, obscenity or a heavy use of dialect or slang. Drug abuse is not an acceptable subject for this genre: nor is any kind of sexual abuse. You are therefore subject to certain limitations and if you think this would cramp your style then you'd be wise not to try.

If, however, you feel you'd like to find out more about both markets, why not write off to a few publishers asking them to send you their guidelines? I have to warn you that in the past it has always been difficult for new writers to break into what is a highly specialised field, but the demand is increasing so much that publishers may well be glad to hear from anyone who has a good idea for a story and is prepared to adapt their style to suit the genre.

Fashions and fads

How can you be sure of being up-to-date when teenage fashions change so rapidly?

The answer is that you can't. That's why it is advisable to avoid being too specific, such as referring to pop records, current crazes, soap operas or even words and phrases that may be in vogue now but will be old hat by the time your book is published. The continuing appeal of jeans for both sexes is a great blessing for writers, but if you want to mention a rock star make sure it's someone whose appeal is likely to last a very long time. It is essential that your dialogue should sound young, natural and lively, but you can achieve this without the use of too much current slang.

Don't try too hard to be trendy. Teenage culture, fed by specialist magazines which are by their very nature ephemeral, is something of a closed book to most adults. Your novel, you hope, will have a far longer shelf life. This does not mean that you need not do any research. You can learn a great deal by watching and listening to teenagers, as well as reading their magazines and watching television programmes intended specifically for them.

It's surprising how little some things change. If you visit a disco you'll find that, apart from the obvious technical innovations, the ritual taking place on the dance floor is as old as the hills. My advice, therefore, is not to worry too much about current fads and fashions. Write the book you want to write and check out the details later. You may be pleasantly surprised how little you have to alter.

One way of avoiding the issue altogether is to set your story back in time. In one of the most popular series ever written for young adults, K.M. Peyton's four Flambards books, Christina is shown growing up against a background of the birth of aviation and the First World War. Surely this disproves yet again the fallacious idea that teenagers only want to read books that mirror their own lives and are set in their own time.

How frank can you be?

No one who reads a newspaper can fail to be aware of the kind of pressures many teenagers are subjected to. Parental abuse, drugs, AIDS, and the dangers of casual sex are all discussed openly in schools and on television. Surely, therefore, the fiction provided for this age group should also deal fully and frankly with these matters?

Some of it does. It entirely depends on the policy of the publishing house concerned. Many are prepared to consider – and may indeed welcome – a book that pulls no punches. Judy Blume, whose books are highly popular with young readers, never flinches from tackling the more basic aspects of life. Her book *Forever* deals frankly with teenage sex; *Are you there, God? It's me, Margaret* describes a young girl's first experience of menstruation.

It is important to bear in mind that young adults, however tough they may appear to be on the outside, are at an emotionally vulnerable age. To offer them problems without the hope of finding a solution would be irresponsible. Be as frank as you want to be; but there should always be – in my opinion at least – a glimmer of light at the end of the tunnel.

A comment given to me by John Escott, author of several books for young adults, puts the whole question into perspective. "I don't think of the people I write for as belonging to any particular age group," he said. "I just assume that what offends me will probably also offend them. So really there's no problem."

If you are seriously interested in writing for this age group I suggest you read David Silwyn William's book on *How to write for Teenagers*, also published by Allison & Busby in this series.

13

NON-FICTION

Non-fiction is a convenient umbrella covering everything that cannot be described as "a story". In a children's library it embraces History, Sport, Nature, Biography, Religion, Science, Jokes and even Poetry. It can deal with complex subjects in brief, as in an encyclopaedia, and quite simple subjects at length, as in an information book. For writers it offers a wonderful opportunity to work in their own special field of interest, and to share that interest with a wide and receptive readership.

The main difference between writing fiction and non-fiction is that you sell non-fiction *before* you write the book. Even a novice writer without an agent can do this successfully and I shall be giving you advice on how to set about it later in this chapter. Then, if you are lucky enough to be commissioned, you work closely with the editor to make sure it conforms to their house style. It is therefore much more of a group effort than a novel, and – provided you make a good job of your first attempt – can lead to more work, often initiated by the publisher.

First, however, you have to get your foot in the door.

Looking for the gaps

The quality of non-fiction books for children has improved beyond recognition in recent years. In the past most factual books were frankly dull, as well as being limited as regards subject matter. Nowadays there is a wide variety of material available on almost every subject you can think of; and most of it is imaginatively written, well-produced and lavishly illustrated.

Almost every subject – therein lies the problem as far as the writer is concerned. Finding a new subject – or even better, a new slant on an old subject – is half the battle. So where do you begin?

Geoffrey Lamb, who has written or edited many educational books, says: "My first published book was a prose anthology for use in schools. I had seen a prose anthology about Children in Literature on the shelves of a local library, and after glancing through it I thought (rather contemptuously) that any fool could do a book like that. Then the thought struck me I ought to try one myself! Eventually, after a good many tries with a good many publishers, Harrap accepted my scheme."

Like Geoffrey Lamb, many non-fiction writers started out as teachers: some, indeed, continue to combine both careers. Textbooks, especially, tend to be written by people actively involved in education, who have studied their subject in depth and know what is required in a classroom situation.

The vast majority of non-fiction books for children, however, are not designed as teachers' instructional aids, but as sources of background knowledge for the child to use by himself. As every teacher knows, there is nothing a child likes better than to be given a project book and told he can write about any subject he chooses. Even a reluctant reader will spend hours poring over information books that may help him to discover what he needs to know.

Information books can be about anything from dinosaurs to computers, but you should try to avoid those areas which have been well and truly covered already. What you are looking for is a topic which, in your opinion, is crying out to have a book written about it. As soon as you have the germ of an idea you should investigate thoroughly the non-fiction shelves of your public or school library, as well as those of your local bookseller, to check that there really is a gap in the market. Even if there is already a book dealing with your topic, you may be able to find a slightly different approach that will enable you to bring in fresh material. When you have a clear picture of what's needed you are ready to start planning your book.

One word of warning: if you do find a gap ask yourself why it's there. Is it because no one else has been brilliant enough to think of it; or because there wouldn't be any demand for the subject? For example, there's no book on historic washing up brushes, but does anybody want one? Remember, it's vital to consider the market.

Research

Having decided on your topic, you come to the most enjoyable part – the acquisition of material. Before approaching a publisher you will need to do some preliminary research so that you can prepare a detailed book proposal. Then, once he gives you the go-ahead, you can get down to it in earnest.

The resources of your local reference library are there to be tapped; and the librarian will, on request, prepare a bibliography of books available so that you can choose which ones you would like them to obtain for you. Also helpful are the bibliographies at the back of other books on the same subject. One reference book you will find invaluable is Ann Hoffman's *Research for Writers*, which will advise you where to go for information.

It is advisable to double-check any facts you may acquire from books, since it is not unknown for one writer to make a mistake which is then passed on to every other writer who uses his work as a source of material. Accuracy is vital. You should never underestimate a young reader's ability to spot any weak areas in your knowledge. Children are highly critical of mistakes and will soon lose faith in a book if they suspect that its author is not master of his subject.

Bear in mind, too, that your book may be used in countries other than your own, which means that any examples or comparisons you make should be as international as possible. You should also avoid giving too many statistics, or referring to current rates of exchange, since these can so quickly become inaccurate. This is a constant hazard for the non-fiction writer; if his book is reprinted he may have to rewrite whole chapters in order to bring his information up-to-date. Even the photographs have to be checked, in case they show buildings that no longer exist, or fail to show a skyscraper where a skyscraper now stands. Gwynneth Ashby, writer of many junior travel books, always takes the precaution of sending her text to be checked by a national of the country she is writing about before allowing it to go to print.

One final word of warning about research: if you are drawing heavily on research from books, take care you don't simply regurgitate other people's words. If you do, the result will be stilted and lacklustre. On the whole it's best to read widely before you start writing, then put away your reference books until you've finished the book and only get them out again to check the facts.

Interviews

It is unlikely, as well as undesirable, that you will be able to do this entirely by reading books: depending on your subject, some kind of practical research will almost certainly have to be undertaken. This may entail visits to factories, museums, public record offices, or even, for the writer of geographical subjects, other countries – all tax deductible, of course!

Generally speaking, experts in any field are only too happy to give you information: there is nothing they like better than being asked to talk about their favourite subject. However, the first question they will ask is who is publishing your book, so it may be best to leave the interviews until you've got a firm commission. If you need to talk to someone at the proposal stage, make it clear that you are only developing an idea.

Before you interview an expert have your questions well prepared, but if they have already thought about what they want to tell you, put your notebook aside and let them talk. You can ask your questions later. If you want to record the interview always ask permission first. Usually people are happy to be recorded since this means there is less chance of inaccuracy. Remember that experts tend to be busy, so don't waste time or drag out the interview too long; and be generous with signed copies to those who have helped you. People appreciate them and enjoy seeing their names in the acknowledgements.

When writing for information don't forget to send a stamped addressed envelope or postage. Charities also appreciate a donation to cover photocopying costs.

Selection of material

By the time you have finished doing your research you will have a mass of material, far more than you need, and this is where your organisational skills come into play. Try to look at the facts through a child's eyes to decide which ones will appeal to readers. Think of the questions children might ask – or, better still, talk to some first and find out what they really want to know.

The key to writing non-fiction is selection. You may in the end be able to use only a fraction of your research; but there is no virtue in cramming a book with facts for their own sake. Deciding what to leave out is just as important as deciding what to put in; and once you have discarded everything that is irrelevant to your theme, you are ready to start knocking what's left into some sort of shape. It may take time and a great deal of trouble to get it right. Be prepared to make changes at every stage of your work. If you establish good relations with your local school you may be able to discuss your ideas with the Head and even test sections of your book on the children. They will soon tell you if they find the text boring or too difficult!

A common mistake is to try to treat a subject too broadly rather than concentrate on a single aspect. Take sport, for example. Clearly you'd have to narrow that down to one particular activity. If you chose tennis, there would be several options open to you. You could take the history of the game; or you could write short biographical studies, with photographs, of the present-day international stars; or concentrate on one particularly distinguished player. To write an instructional book on how to play the game you obviously need to have had coaching experience, in which case you should give details of your qualifications when submitting your proposal to a publisher.

Concept and structure

The next question you should ask yourself is what sort of a book is it going to be? Instructional? Scholarly? Entertaining? The answer may well be a combination of all three, but you need to have the overall concept clear in your mind before you prepare your proposal.

This concept will be determined largely by the way in which you intend the book to be used. If it is designed primarily as an aid for the teacher, then you must take into account the need for flexibility. All teachers teach differently according to their personalities, and may be working anywhere from an inner city area in Sheffield to a farming community in the Outer Hebrides. Fiona Reynoldson, who has written many educational books on her own subject, History, says that she includes plenty of exercises that can be used by hard-pressed teachers if they wish, but warns against suggesting additional work such as building a medieval fort in the playground. Teachers can think up that sort of exercise for themselves!

If, on the other hand, your book is intended for young children to use on their own, or possibly for the older but less able child, you will need to structure it accordingly. Write simply and in short sentences and paragraphs. Break up your text with sub-headings to make it easier for them to grasp the essential facts. If you suggest things to do, make sure they don't involve the use of materials that are difficult to get hold of, or that might be dangerous for children working on their own.

Margery Fisher, in her appraisal of non-fiction for children, *Matters of Fact*, says that an information book should contain fact, concept and *attitude*. In other words, it is just as important for the author to find the right tone of voice when writing non-fiction as it is for fiction. However hungry children may be for the information you can give them, they will soon lose their appetites if it is served up in a flat, colourless way, full of generalisations. Don't be afraid to stamp your own personality on your work. Your enthusiasm for your subject should shine through, enlivening every statement you make. Children are far more likely to warm to a book they feel has been written by a real live person and not by a teaching machine.

For this reason humour is currently very popular in non-fiction. Take, for example, Terry Deary's *The Terrible Tudors* or *The Vile Victorians* in Hippo's *Horrible Histories* series. Or Diana Kimpton's *The Hospital Highway Code*, which informs children in a reassuringly light-hearted way what to expect if they go into hospital. Many writers who fail to break into the non-fiction market do so because they deal with their chosen subject in such a stiff, pedantic style that they fail to make it interesting, let alone entertaining.

When writing for any age group it is important that the text should be clear and informative, so that a child can absorb the information easily, even if the subject matter is difficult. Many educational writers find it helps to build the book around a specific child with whom readers can identify – bearing in mind, of course, the need to maintain a balance between the sexes. If you choose a girl as your central character, you must also show the life of her male counterpart – perhaps her brother? – and try to feature both equally in the illustrations. Either way, it helps if you can look at the subject from a child's point of view, trying to see it as if for the first time rather than coming to it armed with hindsight and preconceived ideas. Another option is to talk directly to the readers, addressing them as "you".

Approaching a publisher

You have found a gap in the market. You have done your preliminary research. You have selected your material and decided on the concept and structure of your book. Right, now you are ready to approach a publisher.

First, of course, you have to find one – and not just any old publisher. Your best bet is to study the non-fiction shelves in your local children's library and see who specialises in the sort of book you have in mind. This will give you a good overall picture, but you need to follow it up by visiting a well-stocked bookshop to see what is *currently* being published. Look for a series your book may slot into. When you have selected about six possible publishers you can make doubly sure by writing to ask them for a catalogue; or you may be able to get hold of one to look at in the library. By now you will have a much clearer idea how your book is likely to fit into their lists – and what the competition is. There's no point in approaching a publisher with a book on his list which would be in direct competition with yours.

The next question is: should you send a query letter first or submit the full proposal?

There are two schools of thought on this one. Some say that it is best to send a query letter together with an outline and sample material, especially if you are a new writer unknown to the publisher. Others say this is a waste of time, causing delay and extra work for both parties, and you may as well submit a full proposal straight away. Whichever course you decide to take, your first communication should look as professional as you can make it. A neat, business-like presentation will open doors that a badly-typed, mispelled letter will find forever closed.

1. The query letter

This should be brief and to the point, giving the title, the subject matter, the age group and the approximate length of the proposed manuscript. You should also state why you think there's a market for your book and explain briefly why you're the perfect person to write it. Try to make your letter lively and enthusiastic rather than formal and stilted, and address it to a specific editor rather than "Dear Sir". A quick telephone enquiry will soon give you the name of the non-fiction editor.

2. A book proposal

A book proposal usually consists of an outline, a sample chapter, a brief curriculum vitae and a covering letter.

The outline can be simply a list of chapter headings; or, better still, the headings plus a list of the topics to be dealt with. For example, when preparing an outline of this book I summarised this chapter as:

Non-fiction

Extensive market research – subject matter – research – concept and structure – approaching a publisher – illustrations – mainly for fun.

In fact, if you look back, you will see that when I came to write the chapter I found it necessary to change the sub-headings slightly.

This doesn't matter. No publisher regards the outline as being carved in stone: it's simply a skeleton waiting to be fleshed out.

The sample chapter is usually the first chapter in the book; but you may prefer to choose a later chapter which you feel confident about and have already researched. This should give the editor an excellent idea of your writing style and how you intend to approach the subject. It will also demonstrate that you know how to pitch the tone of the book to suit your target age group. For this reason you need to take a lot of time and trouble over getting it right. It is going to be this sample chapter that "sells" the book.

Your curriculum vitae should contain all *relevant* information as regards your past career, ie age, education, work experience, qualifications, outside interests, writing courses attended, contacts with children, any expert knowledge you have connected with your chosen subject – and, of course, any writing credits. You may not have had a book published before but you may have written articles for a local or specialist magazine: if so, mention them. Remember, the purpose of this information is to sell your book, so there's no point in stressing the negative aspects such as the number of rejections you've received!

Your covering letter should be as short and concise as possible. There is no need to go into too much detail about the book, or about your past life, since all this will be covered by the outline and your curriculum vitae, but you should mention the availability of photographs or other illustrations, if relevant. Always enclose a stamped addressed envelope – and don't take it too personally if the first publisher you approach turns you down. It may be that they have already commissioned someone else to write on that subject; or it may not fit into their existing series.

Illustrations

All children will choose a book with plenty of pictures in preference to one that is solid text. Illustrations bring a subject to life and, as in picture books, can work with the text to add a new dimension to a child's understanding. No matter how vivid the words you use to describe what a tiger looks like to a child who has never seen one, a picture will do the job twice as well – and in half the time. And if your subject matter is a bit on the dry side, cartoon style illustrations can lighten things up and add a welcome touch of humour.

Gwynneth Ashby says, "Illustrations in project books vary: some have line drawings in addition to colour and black-and-white photographs. If possible take your own photographs, particularly colour, making sure that you take colour slides and not prints."

If you are not a photographer perhaps you can find one with whom you can collaborate; or, failing that, you could visit the picture libraries yourself to find exactly what you want. Once your book has been commissioned professional help will be available and you will work in close liaison with the illustrator or researcher assigned to you.

For drawings you will be expected to provide reference materials where available and check roughs for accuracy. It's well worth collecting suitable reference material during your research, eg photocopies of illustrations from other books, actual objects, or photographs you have taken yourself.

If your subject needs to be illustrated by diagrams and you are not a competent artist, don't worry. Whoever is in charge of the artwork will see that your rough copy is reproduced in a professional way. However the artist chosen by the publisher may have no specialised knowledge of the subject, so if accurate drawings are required to illustrate technical points you will need to draw the roughs carefully and supply a straightforward brief.

Mainly for fun

Not all non-fiction books are, strictly speaking, educational. If you have an inexhaustible supply of jokes, or if you enjoy thinking up puzzles and quizzes, you may like to explore this ever-popular corner of the market.

Another idea worth exploring is that of activity books, both those designed to be used by individual children at home and those intended for classroom use. Again, it is a question of looking for the gaps. Highly popular at the moment are mystery books designed for young would-be detectives, full of picture puzzles, clues to work out and codes to crack. If something like this appeals to you, fine: but you will need to find your own individual approach rather than try to climb on somebody else's bandwaggon.

You should also bear in mind that you are writing for modern children, and the material you produce must reflect the world they live. Recently Scholastic have brought out *The Euro Fun Pack*, which is "an enjoyable introduction to Europe", and *The Green Activity Pack*.

The main intention of these books is to entertain, but that certainly doesn't mean they have no educational value. Any book that demands some kind of active participation from readers will help to develop their mental agility, as well as adding to their store of general knowledge.

To sum up:

1. Look for the gaps.
2. Do your preliminary research.
3. Prepare a detailed outline and a sample chapter.
4. Approach a publisher.
5. Once you've hooked him – start writing!

14

THE PROFESSIONAL TOUCH

At last your book is finished. You've put the final full stop to the final sentence and now you can't wait to send it off to a publisher.
WAIT!
Don't be too hasty. This is the stage that separates the professional from the novice and may well be the deciding factor as to whether or not your story will sell. It is time to rest, recharge your batteries, and take a long cool look at what you have done so far.

A critical eye

First you need to distance yourself from your work. At the moment you are still flushed with the excitement of creation: euphoria has set in and you're convinced you've produced the best children's book since *Treasure Island*. That's only to be expected. If you had not been passionately in love with what you were doing you would not have had the energy to write it. Now you need to be more objective.

I recommend that you put your manuscript away in a drawer and forget about it for at least a week, preferably longer. Do something entirely different, such as gardening, playing the violin or catching up with all the mail you've left unanswered while you were writing. Not until your mind is clear and you feel quite calm and detached are you ready to take your manuscript out of the drawer and settle down to read it with a critical eye.

Has it turned out exactly as you intended?

Well, it may have done, if you happen to be one of those rare people whose minds are so well-organised that they get it right first time. But the chances are that on re-reading your work you will find a lot of rough edges, sentences that could have been better constructed, and whole passages in need of drastic cutting and re-shaping. In which case it would be far better to revise it now, before it goes off to a publisher, than send it half-finished and hope he won't notice there's anything wrong.

Some people may tell you that too much revision can destroy the natural spontaneity of a book, and of course that's the last thing you want. It depends how you interpret the word "revision". In fact what you're aiming to do is iron out all the awkward phrases and clumsy bits of construction so that the book reads smoothly and effortlessly, giving the *illusion* of spontaneity. Therein lies the whole art of writing.

In order to revise your work you have to be ruthlessly self-critical; but before you can start criticising you need to know what are the weaknesses you are looking for.

Here are some of the questions you should ask yourself:

Does the story get off to a good start?
Look again at that all-important first chapter. Is the opening strong enough? Will it catch a young reader's attention?

Are there any dull bits?
Check for stodge. You may be surprised to find how long a particular scene goes on without much happening. If necessary, be prepared to cut large chunks of introspection or superfluous dialogue.

Have I made everything clear?
Maybe you've left out some vital piece of information, assuming that the reader will understand what's happening without being told. Or you may find a sentence that even you, the author, have to read twice before you can make sense of it, so pity the poor reader.

Have I used too many adjectives and adverbs?
Almost certainly. It's a fault most writers have to guard against, the compulsion to qualify nouns and verbs in case they don't have enough impact. Try to choose nouns or verbs that are strong enough to stand alone.

Have I been self-indulgent?
In any book there will be certain passages – usually descriptive – of which you are inordinately fond, but which are totally irrelevant. Or you may have expounded at some length on a subject you feel particularly strongly about, thereby lapsing into preachiness. Or you may have crammed in too many facts and figures rather than waste all that interesting research. If so, cut them out.

Have I over-used certain words?
We all have our pet words, the ones we tend to use far too often. My own particular favourite is "just" as in "I am just looking". Occasionally, if the sentence sounds wrong without it, I allow myself to leave it in; but usually it can be edited out. Others to watch out for are "suddenly", "next", "then", "obviously", "clearly" and "very", but there are many more which you will soon begin to recognise. Sometimes – and there's another one! – there is no alternative, but they should be used sparingly.

Have I checked all my references?
This applies to fiction as well as non-fiction. Memory can play the strangest tricks and even facts you're certain you know can turn out to be wrong. You can't afford to take anything for granted. It's possible that a mistake will be picked up by the editor working on your book: but if you make too many he won't have a very high opinion of your reliability as an author. So check and double-check all your facts.

Have I chosen an appealing title?
A child choosing a book from the library shelf will be drawn partly by the title and partly by the jacket. You may not have much control over the jacket design, but you can make sure that your title contains words that catch the eye and fire the imagination, while at the same time giving some idea of what the book is about.

You may feel, when you have finished revising your work, that you would like to read it aloud to a child or class of children and ask for their opinions. This can be a helpful exercise, especially when it comes to identifying any dull bits – yawns and shuffling feet are the danger signs – but be warned that the comments you receive aren't likely to be very constructive. If children like you they will tell you what they think you want to hear; and even if they say frankly there were parts of it they didn't enjoy, they probably won't be able to tell you why.

Writers' Circles

This brings me to the question of whether or not you would find it helpful to join a Writers' Circle.

If you are lucky enough to have a practical Writers' Circle or Group near to where you live, then I would unhesitatingly advise you to join it. By "practical" I mean one where the members meet frequently to consider each other's work and give constructive criticism. Taking criticism is never easy and often I find myself resisting it strongly; but if several people make the same comment there's a good chance they are right. In any case you will eventually have to show your work to a highly critical publisher, so you may as well get in a little early practice at taking it on the chin.

Often, too, a fresh eye can spot inconsistencies you are incapable of seeing yourself because you are too close. Once I read to my Writers' Group a chapter about a girl and a boy who were lost in the mist on Dartmoor. As it drew near the end one member's expression grew more and more puzzled. When I finished he said, "Fine – but what happened to the dog?" I had been so carried away writing about the girl and boy that I had completely forgotten about their dog, even though I had stated that he was with them when they left home. Can you imagine how agitated my readers would become if they thought – quite wrongly – that the dog had been abandoned on the moors in a swirling mist?

Incidentally, never feel you must preface reading out your work with a humble, "I'm afraid this is only a children's story." Most people can appreciate a good story at any level. In any case, writing for children is not, as we've seen, something for which you need to apologise.

Presentation

It may be true to say that, if you have written a masterpiece, a publisher will overlook the fact that it's badly typed on scruffy paper and full of spelling mistakes – provided, that is, he isn't so put off by its appearance that he refuses to read it! Admittedly, looks aren't everything, but a weary editor will almost certainly choose to take a clean, well-presented manuscript home to read in preference to a near-illegible one.

The final copy should be clearly typed or printed on one side only of good quality A4 paper. Use double spacing throughout, with no extra spaces between paragraphs. All pages must be numbered at the top, either in the centre or at the right-hand corner; and you should leave good margins all round, but especially on the left-hand side. Keep last-minute alterations to a minimum; and if you must change something do so neatly and clearly. The front page should contain the title, the author's name, address and telephone number, and the approximate number of words.

If you are not a good typist it is well worth paying to have your manuscript typed professionally. However, in these days of word processors we can all be good typists, since mistakes can be corrected on the screen before printing. If you are not yet the proud owner of a PC I would strongly recommend you to seek advice about buying one. Yes, it will take you a little time to learn how to use it, but if you are serious about your writing it may well be the best investment you have ever made. Above all else, the copy of your book that lands on the editor's desk needs to be sharp, clear and easy-to-read.

Spelling mistakes are not a mortal sin: nonetheless it's preferable not to make them. Here again the spell-check facility on a PC can be a help: otherwise have a dictionary constantly on hand, and if you're a poor speller ask someone else to check your work before you send it off, just in case.

Punctuation is always tricky because it can vary so much according to fashion, and no matter how careful you are it will probably be changed by your copy-editor. These days, for example, colons and semi-colons are not used nearly so often as they used to be, especially in children's books; and even commas are kept to a minimum. Be warned, too, that we all have our little idiosyncrasies. It was my American editor who cured me of my addiction to dots and dashes. When writing dialogue I used to end practically every speech with either a dash or three dots to indicate that this was an ongoing conversation. Not only was this unecessary, it was also distracting for the reader. She also made me aware how often I used exclamation points when, strictly speaking, they weren't needed. Unfortunately it's all too easy to get into bad habits, which you don't even notice until someone points them out to you. If you are uncertain about punctuation, look at any recently published novel to see how it's done.

Sending your "baby" out into the world

Now comes the moment you have been both longing for and dreading, when you pack up your precious manuscript and send it off.

First make sure you keep at least one copy, preferably two. It is not unknown for manuscripts to be lost in the post or mislaid in a busy publisher's office – and the thought of having to write a book twice is unthinkable.

Should you send it straight to a publisher or try to find an agent?
Most publishers say that it makes no difference whether your manuscript comes to them direct or is filtered through an agent: if it's any good they will sit up and take notice. This may be true; but in practice they are far more likely to read it quickly if it comes to them via a known agent, whereas it could languish for weeks on the slush pile. A good agent will advise you on your work, send it out to publishers he knows are looking for the type of book you've written, and – if it is accepted – negotiate on your behalf the terms of the contract. In my opinion you have nothing to lose by trying one or two agents first: if they show no interest then you can start writing to publishers.

How do you go about finding one?
Names and addresses of agents and publishers are given in the

Writers' and Artists' Year Book and in *The Writer's Handbook*. Selecting the right agent is tricky, unless you happen to hear of one who's specially recommended. This is where it helps if you belong to a Writers' Circle or go to one of the Writers' Workshops or Conferences that may be organised in your area. You can pick up all sorts of useful information that way. When it comes to finding a publisher, you can look in bookshops and libraries to see which publishing houses specialise in the kind of book you have to offer. You should be able to make quite a long list, and then it's a matter of working your way steadily through them.

Should you send a query letter first?
Yes. It's quite possible that a publisher's fiction list may be closed for the time being, in which case there's no point in wasting his time and your postage by sending the complete manuscript until you know he's prepared to read it. Make the letter as brief and business-like as possible – ie don't give him your entire life history and your views on writing in general – but enclose a short synopsis of the story and possibly your curriculum vitae if you think it's relevant. I always think it's a good idea to send a copy of the first chapter as well, because this will give him a far better idea of your writing skill than a brief synopsis. And don't forget to enclose a stamped addressed envelope for his reply.

How should you package it?
This may sound a little unnerving, but it seems that publishers prefer manuscripts that come in the form of loose pages, which is why it's vital to make sure the pages are all clearly numbered. Editors don't like pins or staples and aren't particularly keen on MSS that are clamped into a file. Paper clips are okay, provided they are the flat variety that don't get caught up in other documents. What I usually do is to secure the manuscript with a rubber band and – provided it's slim enough – place it inside an envelope folder. If it's too bulky for a folder I put it inside a plastic bag. The invention of the padded envelope has been a great boon for writers, and if treated with care can be used more than once.

Again, don't forget to send stamps to cover the cost of return postage. And if you want to be certain publishers acknowledge the safe arrival of your manuscript, send a stamped postcard for them to dispatch as soon as they have received it.

How long should you wait for a decision?
Three months is the average "waiting time". After that you either start getting extremely hopeful or begin to wonder if they've lost it; but you may be afraid of upsetting them – possibly at the crucial moment of decision – by demanding that they send your manuscript back. Take comfort: this is a dilemma all writers experience. I consider that after three months you'd be perfectly justified in writing politely to ask if they have come to a decision yet. It may jolt their memories and is unlikely to put them off if they are genuinely enthusiastic about your book.

Is it permissible to send your manuscript to more than one publisher at the same time?
Permissible, yes. But is it advisable? At one time the practice of multiple submissions was frowned upon, but these days it is quite common for an agent to send a manuscript to several publishers at once in order to introduce an element of competition. However, if you don't have an agent and this is your first book you might be better advised to stick to the accepted code of practice – at least, up to the three months' waiting time. After that, if you've had no reply to your follow-up letter, then I reckon you're perfectly justified in offering it elsewhere. This applies particularly to non-fiction, where you cannot afford to hang around too long, especially if your subject is topical.

On bouncing back

Less welcome, even, than an electricity bill or an income tax demand is the sight of your returned manuscript coming through the letter box. You are allowed about half-an-hour of suicidal gloom, after which you have to remind yourself that many successful books have been rejected – some as many as twenty-six times! – and yet have gone on to be best-sellers. Obviously *their* authors didn't sit around and mope.

Before sending it out again, however, it is worth taking another look at it, especially if the publisher had made any comment. For example, he may say that it started well but he found the end disappointing. If, on reflection, you decide that he's right, you would be well advised to try to improve the end before sending it off again. The fact that he has made any comment at all should be regarded as encouraging: at least he hasn't sent it back to you with a printed rejection slip.

This ability to "bounce back" after a rejection requires strength of character. It would be only too easy to give up what often appears to be a hopelessly unequal struggle, trying to get your book published against all the odds. Nobody, it seems, wants to know: they are obviously blind to your qualities as a writer, so what's the point of going on? This is where the real test comes. Are you determined enough to go on until you break through the publication barrier?

When I taught Creative Writing I was often amazed how talented some of the students were, producing work that deserved to be read by a wider public. The fact is, though, that talent alone is not enough: it's the ones who have talent plus stickability who will eventually succeed in getting something published. Paradoxically, you have to develop a certain toughness if you want to survive in the highly commercial world of publishing, while at the same time retaining the sensitivity that is essential to your work. It isn't that you don't care when you're rejected: it's simply that you won't take "no" for an answer – at least, not until you have exhausted all possible outlets.

Undoubtedly luck plays a large part in deciding whether or not your book is accepted. It has to land on the right desk at the right time: everything depends on the editor being on your wavelength. What a gamble!

But that's what gets the adrenalin going. There's always the chance that tomorrow the telephone will ring and someone will say, "We like this book. Can you come and talk to us about it?" And if THAT happens it will take a lot longer than half-an-hour for you to come down from Cloud Nine.

On being flexible

What may bring you back to earth with a bump is the discovery that the editor wants you to make some alterations.

Your initial instinct will be to clutch your manuscript protectively to your chest and say, "No, I don't want to change a thing. I like it just the way it is." My advice is to murmur something non-committal and go home to think about it. The chances are that you will come round to the editor's way of thinking and realise that the changes will be for the better. If, however, you disagree strongly then you must say so, as tactfully as possible, and give your reasons. Once, before commissioning a book, my editor asked me if I could set the story in a different location. I said yes, I could; but it would be an entirely different story and I explained why. She wrote back at once to say that she saw exactly what I meant and please leave the story as it was. Unusually I try to be as flexible as possible, even if it means having to compromise. That doesn't mean you need sacrifice your principles; only that it's unwise to create difficulties over small, unimportant points, thereby earning yourself a reputation as a "difficult author".

One of the trickiest areas of flexibility is the jacket design. As I say above, you may not have much say in the matter, although most editors will send a copy at some stage for your approval – usually when it's too late for you to object! If your book is coming out in hardback, it's a good idea to ask if you can see a "rough" of the jacket before the block is made, so that you have time to spot any glaring inconsistencies. So often you hear stories of artists getting it wrong, such as a showing a girl with fair hair when the text states clearly that she is dark. Not all publishers are open to suggestion, but if you do have an idea about the jacket design then you should mention it early on in your discussions, rather than waiting until it's too late for alterations. There is no guarantee they'll take it up, but if it's good they will certainly bear it in mind.

Be prepared, too, for them to change the title. This has happened to me more times than I care to remember, and it has not always been for the best. If you feel strongly about it, say so; but in the end it's usually the marketing department that has the final word, in which case all you can do is bite the bullet and hope that their judgement is better than yours!

Remember, the relationship you form with your editor is going to be of vital importance, not only where your first book is concerned but also in the way it affects your future work. Your writing career doesn't end with the publication of your first book. On the contrary, it has only just begun.

15

MEETING YOUR READERS

Increasingly, with the practice of holding special "Book Weeks" becoming ever more popular, one of the more pleasurable consequences for a children's writer is being invited to speak to groups of children either in schools or at a local library. I say "pleasurable" because your audience will almost certainly be honest, lively and appreciative, and the feedback you receive on these occasions is invaluable. However there are some do's and don't which it may be helpful to mention.

Ideally, the children will have been well prepared for your visit. Your book has been read to them in class and they may even have done some artwork connected with the story. They will have seen your name in print and been told that they are about to meet a real, live author, so the minute you walk into the room about thirty pairs of eyes will be rivetted to you, curious to see in what way you differ from ordinary mortals. At this point you become uncomfortably aware that something unusual is expected of you and that just being an author isn't enough: you have to be an entertainer as well.

Your approach will differ, of course, according to the age group you are addressing. Very young children soon become restless if you talk *at* them rather than *with* them, and they aren't likely to be held spellbound by someone nattering on about the techniques of writing. Some kind of visual aid is essential, perhaps large-scale drawings of your characters or scenes from the story. This is where the author/illustrator has such an advantage. Shirley Hughes says that children relax immediately when she begins to draw, although it does involve enormous concentration to draw *and* hold an audience at the same time.

She recalls with great affection the time when she used to go

on tour with the late Dorothy Edwards. "I feel I picked up everything I know about addressing a child audience by being there with
Dorothy, drawing pictures while she talked. She had the most natural address to children I've ever encountered – funny, immediate,
never patronising to the slightest degree, but always grown-up,
by which I mean never trying to "come down" to their level,
which some children's authors try to do with disastrous and embar-
rassing results. She had, of course, enormously clear and lively
recall of her own childhood and a marvellous memory for things
other people had told her about theirs. Her love – and respect –
for her child audience was always there."

Shirley Hughes emphasises how important it is for children to
be able to talk back to the speaker, so that it becomes more of a
conversation than a lecture. This can be a problem if you find yourself in a large hall with over fifty children, which means it may
be impossible to hear what those at the back are trying to say –
and that you are having to shout to make yourself audible. If, during your preliminary discussions with the school, you can suggest
that numbers should be limited to about thirty, this will undoubtedly make things easier. Personally, I much prefer to do two
sessions with thirty children than one session with sixty.

When speaking to children of about 8-11 you will find it works
best if you talk about one particular story you have written rather
than about writing in general. If you start by reading short extracts,
so that they get the flavour of the book, and then tell them how
the idea first came to you and how you developed it, you will be
amazed at the range and astuteness of the questions you are asked.

With this age group I generally conclude with a story-building
session, in which I ask children to think up a couple of characters, starting in each case with the name, and then to put those
characters into a situation. Gradually this begins to build into a
story and soon the children are brimming over with suggestions
about what happens next. At this stage it takes all my skill as a
storyteller to maintain some kind of shape and cohesion, and I have
to be prepared for some highly unusual twists and turns of the plot.
As soon as we reach a promising cliffhanger, I say, "Right, now
it's over to you. Go away and finish it off." Some children will
do exactly what you tell them; some will painstakingly reproduce
everything you've said, finishing it off with one short sentence;

and some will write an entirely different story. None of this matters. The aim is not only to provide a starting point, but also to ensure that your visit may bear some fruit and not be merely an enjoyable diversion.

Talking to older children requires a different technique again. Some kind of description of your work – not too lengthy – will be necessary at the beginning, partly to break the ice and partly to clear up any misconceptions they may have about writers in general. After that it helps if you can get a dialogue going, which means that you need to establish some kind of rapport with your audience. Adolescents are often reluctant to speak out in front of their peers for fear of sounding foolish, so somehow you have to let them know that you don't mind how obvious or elementary their questions may be – you are prepared to answer anything. Once you've created the right kind of atmosphere you will be surprised how genuinely interested they are in the whole business of writing. The chances are that some have literary aspirations themselves and are therefore genuinely interested to know how best to start on a writing career.

There are of course certain hazards lying in wait for the unwary speaker, such as the child who has a nose-bleed in the middle of your talk which totally disrupts everyone's concentration; or the visual aids you've blu-tacked to the wall behind you suddenly descending on your head while you are in mid-flow. On the whole, disciplinary problems don't occur, since there is always a teacher present to frown menacingly at persistent fidgeters or even, in extreme cases, to eject them from the hall. I remember one particular occasion, however, when I was invited to speak to a group of 7-9 year olds. My talk went well, but afterwards the Head asked if I'd mind speaking again to a class of infants who had been *so* disappointed not to hear me. What else could I say but yes? She then showed me into a room of saucer-eyed five-year-olds and LEFT ME TO IT! Totally unprepared, I did the only thing possible and told them a story, while at the same wiping a few noses and breaking up the odd fight that threatened to break out. Twenty-five minutes later I was relieved – in more ways than one – by the class teacher, by which time I had a strong suspicion that I'd been conned into baby-sitting while the staff took a tea-break. In all fairness I must say this has only happened to me once: usually the organisation is excellent and the staff very mindful of a writer's comfort and sensibilities.

Do children really get anything out of these visits? You can only hope they receive some sort of stimulation, or at the very least realise that books are written by ordinary, accessible people and not by remote beings living in ivory towers.

For the writer, of course, the rewards are considerable – and I don't mean only the financial ones, although these days most schools are able to pay speakers a respectable fee, thanks to funding from regional Arts Councils. But here is a unique opportunity to find out from your readers what they like about your books and what they don't like. Be prepared for total honesty, especially from the very young. And don't just pay attention to the extrovert, bright, articulate children, even though they may be the ones you notice most in the group. Look out for the ones who listen raptly but keep quiet when you ask for questions and hang back at the end when the others push forward, clamouring for you to sign your name on scrappy bits of paper. It is these children I often feel drawn to most, because the chances are that they are the *bookish* ones; and therefore they remind me of myself at that age.

And at the end of a visit, if a small girl with serious eyes tugs and your sleeve and whispers, "I liked your book. I've read it twice" – well, that's when you know it's all been worth while.

READING LIST

The following is a selection of books mentioned in the text which may serve as a useful guide to further reading.

Children's Fiction:

Janet and Allan Ahlberg: *The Jolly Postman* (Heinemann)
Malorie Blackman: *Hacker* (Doubleday)
John Burningham: *Mr Gumpy's Outing* (Jonathan Cape)
Beverley Cleary: *Ramona the Pest* (Hamish Hamilton/Puffin)
Babette Cole: *Princess Smartypants* (Hamish Hamilton)
Michael Coleman: *Triv in Pursuit* (Bodley Head)
Robert Cormier: *I am the Cheese* (Gollancz)
Gillian Cross: *The Great Elephant Chase* (OUP)
Paula Danziger: *The Pistachio Prescription* (Heinemann/Pan Piper)
C. Day Lewis: *The Otterbury Incident* (Bodley Head/Puffin)
Anita Desai: *The Village by the Sea* (Heinemann/Puffin)
Farrukh Dhondy: *Come to Mecca* (Collins/Fontana Lions)
Dorothy Edwards: *My Naughty Little Sister* (Methuen/Magnet)
Anne Fine: *Goggle-Eyes* (Hamish Hamilton/Puffin)
Anne Fine: *Stranger Danger* (Hamish Hamilton Gazelles)
Alan Garner: *Elidor* (Collins/Puffin)
Alan Garner: *The Owl Service* (Collins/Fontana Lions)
Adèle Geras: *The Tower Room* (Hamish Hamilton)
Shirley Hughes: *An Evening at Alfie's* (Bodley Head)
Shirley Hughes: *Dogger* (Bodley Head/Fontana Lions)
Shirley Hughes: *Moving Molly* (Bodley Head/Fontana Lions)
Pat Hutchins: *Rosie's Walk* (Bodley Head/Puffin)
Terry Jones: *The Saga of Erik the Viking* (Pavilion)
Diana Kimpton: *The Bear that Santa Claus Forgot* (Scholastic)
E.L. Konigsburg: *From the Mixed-up Files of Mrs Basil E. Frankweiler* (Macmillan)

Tessa Krailing: *Alberta the Abominable Snowthing* (Hamish Hamilton Antelope)

Tessa Krailing: *A Dinosaur called Minerva* (Hamish Hamilton/ Puffin)

Tessa Krailing: *Message from Venus* (Hutchinson/Red Fox)

Tessa Krailing: *Only Miranda* (Hamish Hamilton/Puffin)

David McKee: *Not Now, Bernard* (Andersen/Sparrow)

Marjorie Newman: *Green Monster Magic* (Hodder & Stoughton Roosters)

K.M. Peyton: *Flambards* (OUP/Puffin)

Elfrida Vipont: *The Elephant and the Bad Baby* (Hamish Hamilton)

Cynthia Voigt: *Homecoming* (Collins/Lions)

E.B. White: *Charlotte's Web* (Hamish Hamilton/Puffin)

Valerie Wilding: *Prince Vince and the Case of the Smelly Goat* (Hodder Story Books)

General

Carmel Bird: *Dear Writer* (Virago)

Dorothea Brande: *Becoming a Writer* (Macmillan)

Dianne Doubtfire: *The Craft of Novel-Writing* (Allison & Busby)

Ann Hoffman: *Research for Writers* (A & C Black)

Strunk & White: *The Elements of Style* (Macmillan)

David Silwyn Williams: *How to Write for Teenagers* (Allison & Busby)

INDEX

INDEX